Main

Drones

FOR DUMMIES®

A Wiley Brand

by Mark LaFay

FOR DUMMIES®

A Wiley Brand

Drones For Dummies®

Published by **John Wiley & Sons, Inc.,** 111 River Street, Hoboken, NJ 07030-5774, www.wiley.com

Copyright © 2015 by John Wiley & Sons, Inc., Hoboken, New Jersey

Published simultaneously in Canada

Contents at a Glance

Table of Contents

Introduction

They go by several names — unmanned aerial vehicle, remotely piloted vehicle, and remote controlled aircraft — but the one you've probably heard the most is *drone*. Drones have become a household name first due to their use in warzones around the world, and then more so because of their use for domestic and international spying. Now drones are becoming deeply embedded into pop culture because advancements in technology have made it possible for the average Joe like you and me to buy or build a small unmanned aircraft, or drone.

In the early days of remote-controlled flight, you had only the option of one type of aircraft, the model airplane. This was due largely to the limitations of the technology of the day. Today, thanks to the advancements made in smartphones, the technology needed to make advanced aircraft like quad-copters exists. The computers and sensors that make smartphones detect orientation and motion are used in quadcopters, and other drones, to allow them to take-off vertically, hover in place, move side to side, and do all sorts of aerial maneuvers.

Although the technology has advanced quite a bit since the early days of remote flying, you still need to have a level of skill to enjoyably and success-fully pilot a drone. This book gives you the background and information you need, in a somewhat lighthearted approach, to purchase your own drone and set off into the wild blue yonder.

About This Book

Like most of the *For Dummies* books, this book is not intended necessarily to be read beginning to end. Each chapter is written in a way that you could jump around from chapter to chapter without being confused. That said, it would be smart for you to at least start with the first few chapters so that you can get a feel for drones by first taking a glimpse at their history and how they are being used by governments around the world today. Jump from the evolution of model aircraft into modern day drones and how hobby flyers like yourself are using them for work and play today.

The goal for this book is to get you all the information you need to get airborne safely. Sample chapters in this book include:

- Getting familiar with drones
- Picking the drone that is right for you
- Picking the camera that best fits your needs
- Setting up your drone
- Staying safe with your drone
- Knowing the law
- Controlling your drone
- Flight basics
- Capturing beautiful stills and video

Treat this book as a reference piece. If you are writing a report for school on drones, this book will be wildly helpful. If you need a handy field guide when you go out to fly your drone, this books is for you. While I would like to think that my writing could make any subject matter as intriguing as the *Harry Potter* series, I am not one to kid myself. Read this book in chunks and refer to it often. This book is to help you get airborne with your drone, but the only way you will be an expert pilot is by practicing.

Foolish Assumptions

When writing this book, I tried to not make any silly assumptions that you, the reader, would have existing knowledge of drones. For that reason this book covers a lot of ground starting with the history of drones and quickly navigating into now. I also didn't assume that you already purchased a drone, and therefore this book covers how to shop online.

If you have done any research on drones, you may have noticed that there is an expanding marketplace of different drones, and not just aerial drones. This book does not assume that you own any one particular drone, and therefore, it is written in a manner that considers several different types of drones. The book focuses mainly on what are currently the most popular brands and models of drones available today.

In all my attempts to not assume anything about you, I did assume just this one thing. I assumed that you would not be taking the ultra-hobbyist route by building your own custom drone using kits and parts available on the

Internet. This book assumes that you intend to shop for ready-made drones that are almost ready to fly right out of the box. I also assumed that you had some experience using a computer and the Internet.

This book covers a lot of ground, and my goal is that by the end of this book you will have:

- ✔ Confidently chosen a drone.
- ✔ Familiarized yourself with how your drone works.
- ✔ Built checklists for preparing for flight and wrapping up flight.
- ✔ Identified your own best practices for caring for your drone.
- ✔ Gotten comfortable with federal, state, and local laws governing your drone.

How This Book Is Organized

This book is broken into five main parts, each of which is written about a specific aspect of drones.

Part I: Getting Started with Drones

There are a lot of different names for unmanned aerial vehicles. The term *drone* can be somewhat deceiving because it insinuates something that does not have a pilot but rather flies autonomously. Explore the history of drones so that you can get a vision for the future. If you haven't purchased a drone, get a quick overview of the different features available with drones today so that you can buy the drone right for you. When you get flying, you may be the only person you know with a drone. Learn how to find and connect with other enthusiasts so that you can get your wings faster, learn how to do your own repairs, and make friends with other people fascinated by the boundless open skies.

Part II: Before You Fly

The most popular drones today come with very little assembly required, but you still need to understand what all the different pieces and parts are for so that you are familiar with your drone in the event you ever need to repair or replace parts. Understanding how your drone works will also help keep you safe. You get information in this part that will help keep you safe from unnecessary accidents. Last, the world of drones is evolving and growing rapidly, which is causing the FAA to step in and figure out a way to manage the increasing congestion in our skies. Know the existing law and how to stay legal with your drone.

Part III: The Miracle of Flight

There is a lot of technology that goes into getting a drone airborne. In order to fly, you should understand how you will control your drone and the limitations of that technology. Not to mention, flying a drone isn't like driving a car. Directional control is vastly different with a multi-rotor drone. You will see how to orient and steer your drone in several flight modes. This part will also show you how to set yourself up for success by choosing the right location and time to fly and help you take a methodical approach to flight preparation with your pre-flight checklist.

Part IV: Aerial Photos and Videos

While most hobby flyers fly drones for the sheer enjoyment of flight, most drone owners purchase their drones for taking pictures and video from an aerial vantage point. This part contains chapters that will help you configure your camera for great pictures and video. Explore the importance of light and its impact on how you set up your camera. Get some tips and tricks for making sure you have clear photos and video footage by reducing vibration and shake caused by turbulent flight. Last, explore different software that is available for editing pictures and video and sharing them with friends and family across the web.

Part V: The Part of Tens

This book wraps up with the traditional *For Dummies,* "The Part of Tens." Each chapter is comprised of ten topics or items. Chapters include lists of things you shouldn't do with your drone, as well as a list of things you could do with your drone to make money (assuming the FAA clears the way for lawful commercial use of drones).

Icons Used in This Book

As you read this book, you'll see icons in the margins that indicate material of interest (or not, as the case may be). This section briefly describes each icon in this book.

The tips in this book give you quick insights in how to better use your drone. This includes safety suggestions, maintenance ideas, and techniques on how to maximize your experience using your drone.

At the risk of sounding like an alarmist, anything marked with a warning is something you should pay close attention to. Proceed with caution if you must proceed at all.

Whenever you see this icon, think *advanced* tip or technique or technical information that is helpful and insightful but not mission critical. Feel free to skip these bits of information, but it won't hurt to read them.

If you don't get anything else out of a particular chapter or section, remember the material marked by this icon. This text will remind you of meaningful content that you should file away. This might also remind you of something already covered that is useful again.

Beyond the Book

A lot of extra content that you won't find in this book is available at www.dummies.com. Go online to find the following:

✔ **Online articles covering additional topics at**

www.dummies.com/extras/drones

✔ **The Cheat Sheet for this book is at**

www.dummies.com/cheatsheet/drones

Here you will find quick-reference information that might come in handy when you're in a pinch.

✔ **Updates to this book, if we have any, are available at**

www.dummies.com/updates/drones

Where to Go from Here

You didn't buy this book to use it as a coaster, so I suggest you start with the first chapter. Take a gander at where drone technology has been and where it is headed. There is a lot of information strewn about this book, but don't get overwhelmed by it all.

If you have any questions about drones or drone flight, or if you simply want to drop me a line to say hello, my email is marklafay@gmail.com. I respond to all non-spam emails that I get. If you have questions, I will do my best to respond in a timely manner or forward your contact information on to someone who can help.

If you want a mental break from your reading, feel free to check out some other things that I'm working on that are not related to drones: http://mylectio.com or http://roust.community.

But don't get too distracted. Get busy reading so that you can get busy flying!

Part I
Getting Started with Drones

In This Part . . .

- Getting to know your drone
- Selecting a drone
- Choosing a camera
- Getting help

Chapter 1

Drones 101

In This Chapter

▶ Getting a brief history of drones

▶ Knowing the various types of drones

▶ Understanding the different uses for drones

*I*n this chapter, you take a close look at various types of drones and their applications. You gain an understanding of the differences between drones, UAVs, and RC devices. You even see how drones are used in modern warfare, as well as how they were used in world wars.

Many different types of drones are available for the general public. In this chapter, you see the differences between planes, helicopters, multi-copters, and tiltrotors. You get a glimpse of how average Joes are using drones for hobby flying, aerial video, and aerial photography. You even get a look at how drones are being used for commercial purposes by high-flying drone companies.

Before the chapter kicks off, please make sure that your seatbacks and tray tables are in their upright and locked positions. Ensure your carryon is stowed under the seat in front of you, and your seatbelt is securely fastened low and across your waist. It's time for take-off!

What Are Drones?

When you hear the word *drone*, what is the first thing that comes to mind? If you're like most people, you have visions of military jet-powered aircraft taking out bad guys in a warzone. Or maybe you think of a helicopter hovering outside your home gathering surveillance footage of your mom's secret meatloaf recipe. A high-powered, very high-tech, unmanned aircraft is what probably comes to mind, as shown in Figure 1-1.

Source: U.S. Navy photo by Photographer's Mate 2nd Class Daniel J. McLain

Figure 1-1:
High-tech
drones.

The term *drone* is somewhat misleading when used to describe the high-flying marvels of modern technology. In reality, drones were not always so high-tech. Drones date back as far as the mid 1800s, when the Austrians used balloons filled with bombs to attack Venice. The balloons were launched with a trajectory but there were no advanced piloting controls to guide them to their intended destination. Drones also appeared in the 1900s when they were used by the American military for target practice as a mode of training troops.

It wasn't until the 1930s that remotely piloted vehicles, RPVs for short, were developed. RPVs were first rolled out to train anti-aircraft gunners going into World War II. They were later used to carry out attack runs on Nazi Germany. Remotely Piloted Vehicles are unmanned aircraft that are controlled by a pilot or piloting system located outside of the vehicle. Figure 1-2 shows a World War II era RPV.

RPVs are high-tech versions of the hobbyist's remote controlled (RC) aircraft. Remote controlled aircraft are aerial vehicles that are controlled by a ground operator using a handheld piloting system that communicates using radio frequencies. Hobbyists around the world have been flying RC planes since the '40s and '50s.

Source: Encyclopedia of Astrobiology, Astronomy, and Space Flight: Kettering Bug

Figure 1-2:
World War
II era RPV.

Unmanned Aerial Vehicle, or UAV, is the term most commonly used today to described what the world has come to know as *drones*. UAVs can be controlled using a milieu of high-tech communication protocols like GPS and other satellite communications. UAVs can be remotely piloted by a human, team of humans, or a computerized piloting system. UAVs can also be fully autonomous. How's that for artificial intelligence? Autonomous UAVs are given instructions and then they take off, fly, carry out orders, and land. All without the assistance of humans.

Other terms used to describe drones include remotely piloted aircraft (RPA), remotely operated aircraft (ROA), unmanned aircraft system (UAS), and just recently the FAA (Federal Aviation Administration) adopted the term Unmanned Aircraft (UA) to describe aircraft without flight crew. For the sake of consistency throughout this book, and to be congruent with current trends and vernacular, we will use the term *drone* to describe the high-tech consumer and commercial drones that we all know and love.

Drones and the Military

Drones have played a role in the theater of war for over a century. From the bomb-filled balloons of the 19th century to modern drones that resemble something from science fiction, drones have evolved as they have taken center stage in modern warfare and domestic security operations. Currently, the CIA uses drones primarily to carry out surveillance, although they have some authority to use drones to carry out strikes. The U.S. Armed Forces use drones to carry-out surveillance and combat missions and the department of homeland security uses drones to monitor the American borders.

The U.S. Government currently uses and is testing several high-tech drones, called unmanned aerial systems, or UAS, for short. The following sections offer a brief description and photo of each of the UAS.

General Atomics Predator

The Predator drone was first conceived in the early 1990s but didn't actually see use by the federal government until the mid to late '90s. It was originally used for surveillance and reconnaissance but later was fitted with a combat payload, primarily Hellfire missiles which are an air-to-surface, 100 lbs., rocket-powered missile. The predator's remote piloting system has evolved greatly since the '90s. Advancements in satellite technology has made it possible to manage remote takeoff, landing, and flight from thousands of miles away. There are several hundred predators in use by the U.S. Air Force (USAF) and the CIA but they will be slowly phased out and replaced by the newer version, the Reaper. Figure 1-3 shows the USAF's Predator drone.

General Atomics Reaper

The Reaper is the newest evolution of the famed predator drone. It is faster, more powerful, and more capable in surveillance and combat scenarios. The reaper can fly for 42 hours without a munitions payload and 12 hours with a full munitions payload. The reaper is also capable of carrying several different arms such as laser guided bombs, air-to-surface missiles like the Hellfire, and it will soon be capable of carrying and using air-to-air attack missiles for aerial combat. The Reaper is staked with surveillance capabilities and is rumored to be able to read a license plate from a distance of 2 miles. The advancements in technologies have made the reaper a prime candidate for domestic surveillance, disaster assistance, border monitoring, and homeland security. Figure 1-4 shows the USAF's Reaper drone.

Source: U.S. Air Force photo/Lt Col Leslie Pratt

Source: United States Air Force photo by Senior Airman Larry E. Reid Jr.

Elbit Systems Hermes 450

The Department of Homeland Security and the U.S. Armed Forces use the Hermes 450 primarily for surveillance and reconnaissance. The Hermes 450 can fly at high-altitudes for extended periods of time, making it extremely useful for monitoring large stretches of open territory. The Hermes has yet to be fit with a munitions payload to allow it to have attack capabilities in a combat scenario. Figure 1-5 shows the Department of Homeland Security's Hermes 450 drone.

Figure 1-5:
Department of Homeland Security's Hermes 450.

Source: Gerald L. Nino.

Northrup Gruman Global Hawk

First developed in 1998, the Global Hawk went through several revisions before it made its debut in the U.S. Air Force's arsenal of surveillance tools. The Global Hawk set several world records, one of which being the first unmanned aerial vehicle to cross the Pacific Ocean when it flew from Edwards Air Force Base to RAAF Base Edinburgh in Australia. The flight totaled more than 8200 miles. The Global Hawk also set endurance records by flying for more than 33 hours at altitudes topping 60,000 feet. The Global Hawk is primarily used for global surveillance. Figure 1-6 shows the Global Hawk long-range drone.

Source: U.S. Air Force photo by Bobbi Zapka

Figure 1-6:
The
Northrup
Gruman
Global
Hawk.

Boeing X-37B

Originally developed by Boeing for NASA, the X-37B is classified as an Orbital Test Vehicle or (OTV). The USAF has conducted three missions with the X-37B and has thus far been very secretive on the test missions as well as the intended uses of the X-37B. The most recent flight of the X-37B saw it remain in low orbit for 674 days before being guided back to Vandenberg Air Force Base in California. The X-37B is nearly 30 feet in length and 10 feet in height. Its orbital cruising speed is slightly over 17,000 miles per hour. Figure 1-7 shows the Boeing X-37B.

Smaller drones

The U.S. Armed Forces also use small drones for carrying out battlefield reconnaissance, laser target for missile strikes, and general surveillance. Smaller drones can be launched by hand and remotely piloted using GPS or by first person view. These systems can carry out orders with or without human intervention, making them excellent options for autonomous, constant surveillance.

Figure 1-7:
The
Classified
Boeing
X-37B,
Orbital Test
Vehicle.

Domestic drone surveillance

Drones have been heavily used overseas in conflict zones to monitor military threats, terrorist activity, combat zones, and so-on. But the technology is coming home and being used, and that has a lot of people up in arms. Currently, the U.S. government is using drone technology to monitor its borders. Homeland Security and Customs and Immigration are also using drones to find individuals in distress in remote areas along our southern borders with Mexico and northern borders with Canada.

As drone technology continues to evolve, it will likely be used to monitor for domestic criminal activity, and homegrown terrorist activity. Drone technology isn't only for crime prevention, border security, and domestic espionage. Drones are also proving to be very helpful in locating and mapping forest fires, tracking migratory patterns of wild life, search and rescue, and so-on.

The legality of government surveillance with drone technology is still in debate on the federal level, leaving it up to the states to draft their own legislation on how drone usage can be an invasion of privacy. I discuss the legality of drone usage at greater depth In Chapter 7.

Growth in Consumer Drones

While the majority of the world's media pines over the plight of modern warfare with unmanned aerial war machines, a bigger story is brewing elsewhere in the world. The booming consumer drone industry is doing just that, booming! The consumer drone industry is a relatively new industry and growing at an estimated rate of 15–20% annually. Ironically enough, in the United States, arguably the largest consumer market in the world, the FAA has yet to release an updated set of laws to make commercial use of drones legal. They've also not outlined any sort of legislation necessarily making it illegal (more on that in Chapter 7). When a clear set of legal operating guidelines are released, there is no telling where the drone market might go.

Part of the reason for the boom is that advances in technology have made it easier for high-end hardware and software to be developed and proto-typed at a lower cost. These lower prices make it easier for a large amount of people to gain access to a product, but the real driver behind the surge in drone popularity is in the uses for drones. Drones have attracted more than just model airplane hobbyists and flight hobbyists. The technology advances in flight technology, flight modes, and controls along with the advancements in portable photography and video technology has caused an explosion with amateur and professional photographers and videographers. Who needs high-end video cranes when you can couple a small action camera, like a GoPro, with a drone, as shown in Figure 1-8.

Source: bjoern.gramm/Creative Commons

Figure 1-8: Drone with a GoPro action camera.

The growth in drone popularity can also be seen in the number of drone companies that launched in 2014 and secured funding by launching crowdfunding campaigns that spread virally across the internet. (*Crowdfunding* is the practice of funding a project or venture by raising many small amounts of money from a large number of people, typically via the Internet.)

Hexo+ raised $1.3 million, Airdroids raised $1.36 million, Robot Dragonfly raised $1.14 million, and Indianapolis-based Airdroids raised nearly $1 million for their compact Pocket Drone.

There are several types of drones currently available for purchase by consumers. These types include planes or gliders, helicopters, multi-copters or multi-rotors, and tiltrotors. The following sections discuss each type in detail.

Planes

Remote controlled airplanes have been around for quite some time in the model aircraft world. These devices achieve flight through horizontal takeoff, meaning they gain speed across the ground until enough air moves across the wings to force the plane off the ground and into the air.

Planes also land horizontally, and since their ability to remain airborne requires forward momentum, they do not have the capability to hover in place or move vertically. Planes and gliders can only, and always must, move forward.

Figure 1-9 shows an airplane drone.

Figure 1-9:
Airplane
drone.

Helicopters

These aircraft have two sets of propellers, often referred to as *rotors*. The main rotor is used to create lift to get the aircraft airborne and thrust to move the aircraft forward. The second rotor is used for directional control and stability of the helicopter. Because helicopters do not require thrust to become and remain airborne, they can move forward, backward, and strafe.

Strafing means moving side to side without changing your directional orientation. For example, you facing forward sidestep to the right or left. This movement is called strafing.

Figure 1-10 shows a helicopter drone.

Figure 1-10:
Helicopter
drone.

Multi-copters

If helicopters have two rotors then a multi-copter has more than two. One of the benefits to having a multi-copter, also referred to as a multi-rotor, is that the mechanics involved with flight controls are much simpler. The directional control of a multi-copter is handled by adjusting the speed of each rotor. Multi-copters are the most common commercial drones because of their ease of construction and control. Figure 1-11 shows a multi-copter drone.

Figure 1-11:
Multi-copter
drone.

Tiltrotors

Tiltrotors function in a manner that appears to be a cross between planes and helicopters. On these aircraft, the rotors are positioned above the aircraft to allow for vertical takeoff. The rotors slowly shift forward (toward the nose of the aircraft) as the aircraft gains momentum. This changes the roll of the rotors from creating the lift for vertical takeoff, to creating the thrust thus making the wings responsible for creating the lift. Currently, there are no commercially available tiltrotor drones. Figure 1-12 is a picture of a tiltrotor aircraft.

Figure 1-12:
Tiltrotor
aircraft.

Source:United States Coast Guard, PA3 Bridget Hieronymu

Popular Uses for Drones

In the United States, the organization that controls all air traffic (private and commercial) is the FAA, which stands for the Federal Aviation Administration. In 2012, the U.S. Congress passed a law requiring the FAA to issue rules for legalizing the commercial usage of drones in the United States by September of 2015. Currently, drone usage is protected under the FAA's regulations pertaining to recreational and hobby uses as long as the drone is under 55 lbs.

With no good way of monitoring or policing drone usage, however, there have been many private individuals, companies, farmers, small businesses, and so on that have begun using drones to help them get work done faster, smarter, and at lower risk and liabilities. The following sections describe the most common domestic uses for drones.

Remote sensing

Drones can carry sensing equipment to assist with any number of functions. Geological surveying, agriculture, archeology, and several other industries can benefit greatly from the myriad of sensors that can be packed into a drone. Here are just a few examples of how the agricultural industry, for example, uses aerial sensors:

- Drones can use Lidar to measure the height of crops. *Lidar* is a remote sensing technology that measures distance by illuminating an object with a laser (near-infrared or UV) and then measuring what is reflected back.

- Heat sensors detect the temperature of livestock, the presence of water, water temperature, and for surveillance and emergency response (if someone is injured in a remote field away from heavy equipment).

- Multi-spectral instruments can count plants (crop density), check the health of plants, and even assess water quality.

- Visual spectrum sensors make it possible to survey and map land.

- Biological sensors can be used to take air quality readings and check for the presence of specific micro-organisms or organic compounds.

Commercial aerial surveillance

When you hear surveillance, chances are good that you think about security cameras designed to catch lawbreakers. Or possibly spying and monitoring of your personal movements and actions. Here are just a few ways that aerial surveillance can be helpful:

- Farmers use drones to monitor livestock on vast spreads of land.

- Fire departments can use drones to track and map wild fires.

- Private companies can use drones to monitor their infrastructure such as pipelines, buildings, and so on.

- Using drones to inspect power lines, towers, tall structures like chimneys and roofs would save businesses vast amounts of money and would reduce liability exposure from having humans in harm's way.

Commercial and motion picture filmmaking

In 2014, the Motion Picture Association, backed by seven companies, petitioned the FAA to allow the use of drones in video and filmmaking. Drones dramatically reduce the cost associated with gathering action or aerial footage that up until now would require expensive equipment like booms and dollies or even helicopters or other manned aircraft. In September of 2014, the FAA issued permits to six film studios for the use of drones in filmmaking. Drones are also being used to gather footage in sporting events because of their ability to maneuver into locations that cable-suspended cameras cannot reach. Most recently, drones were used to gather footage of the skiing and snowboarding events in the 2014 Sochi Winter Olympics.

Oil, gas, and mineral exploration

With the help of specific electromagnetic sensors, drones can be used to gather geological information to help geophysicists identify and better approximate the location and presence of minerals, oil, and natural gas.

Disaster relief

The milieu of sensors that can be packed into a drone can be used to help locate and save life in the midst of natural disasters. Drones can be used to gather and deliver medical samples, supplies, and medicine to remote or otherwise unreachable areas in a disaster zone. Drones can also use infrared sensors to detect humans by their heat signature which is helpful in search and rescue scenarios.

Real estate and construction

Drones have made it possible to survey land and gather information at job sites. Realtors, developers, and builders have also begun using drones to gather video and imagery for home and building inspections and marketing materials to assist the selling process.

Recreational use

Needless to say, drones can be extremely useful devices for a plethora of applications ranging from agriculture to national security. However, you can't forget that drones are also really fun to use, which is probably why you are reading this book in the first place! The miracle of flight is something that has fascinated man for millennia, so it's no wonder that hobby flight enthusiasts have been tinkering with flying machines since the late 1800s.

The good news is that personal and hobby use of drones is perfectly legal in the United States. Recreational flying can be done anywhere but is best if done in open locations so that you can always see your aircraft. This is called *line-of-sight flying*. Attaching a camera to your drone is also a lot of fun for gathering beautiful imagery and video of the world around you.

Until the emergence of drones, to take aerial photos or videos, you needed a really tall ladder or a friend with a helicopter/plane to be able to capture the footage. A word of caution, be careful of who, what, and where you take photos and video with your drone. Privacy is a major concern for many people. Chapter 7 touches on some laws and etiquette for flying your drone.

Hobby groups and flying clubs exist all around the globe; plugging into a group is a great way to meet other people passionate about flying. It's also a great way to learn how to fly, learn new techniques, service and maintain your aircraft, and more.

High-Flying Drone Companies

As the drone market continues to explode over the next several years and decades, there will be numerous companies getting into the fray. Currently there are several companies making a lot of noise in the world of unmanned aerial vehicles. You may find it worthwhile to check them out so that you can be in the know on what's going on in drone town.

Google

Google X is a secretive department within Google that's sole purpose is to develop major revolutionary technology. Several initiatives have already become public out of the Google X department, including self-driving cars, Project Wing, and Glass. But the most relevant is Project Wing, Google's automated drone program. Project Wing has become a little more public now that Google has begun testing in remote areas of Australia. Their drone model is designed for long-range, low-energy delivery of materials to remote areas. It is also likely to evolve as they continue to test and innovate.

DHL

DHL is a major global package delivery service based out of Germany. They recently announced that they have begun using their *Parcelcopter* to conduct delivers of medical supplies to a German island. The flight is largely automated through computer controls and it takes roughly 15 minutes each-way and is primarily a long-term test of the new technology. Their long-term vision is to use drone technology to service customers in remote and inaccessible areas.

Amazon

Amazon is one of the largest e-retailers in the world. Their growth is attributed largely to the leadership of CEO Jeff Bezos. Amazon recently unveiled their drone delivery program called *Prime Air,* which aims to get packages into the hands of customers in 30 minutes or less. The Prime Air delivery service was developed in Amazon's next generation R&D lab and is poised for launch in 2015 when the FAA officially puts into place legislation governing commercial UAV usage.

Facebook

Facebook is another household name that has opted to get into the drone business. Facebook's primary motivator, however, is to create a system for delivering Internet access to remote areas of the world that do not yet have access to the Internet. Facebook is working to create ultra-light, solar powered planes that can fly almost indefinitely broadcasting ultra-high wireless signals to these parts of the world. What's exciting about this is the potential to revolutionize wireless communications.

GoPro

GoPro is an action camera company that exploded on the scene by offering great quality video solutions for action sports enthusiasts regardless of their environment. GoPro cameras are used in pretty much every action sport. They have water proof housings, capture high quality footage, and they are small enough to fit on a headband or attached to the body of a drone. GoPro cameras and drones go together like peanut butter and jelly. So much so that GoPro is planning to release their own drone by 2016! More on the camera itself in Chapter 3.

Chapter 2

Picking the Drone That's Right for You

*S*hopping for a drone can be a daunting task. There are several types of drones to choose from, with jargon-rich names like DJI Phantom 2 Vision, or Parrot AR Drone 2.0. What's more, you won't find many physical locations designed specifically for trying before you buy. And there also are several different one-off startup companies out there offering great products, but they aren't grouped into one location. You need to do some work to ensure that you buy the drone that best suits your needs.

Don't worry, you don't have to assume the crash position before we even get airborne! This chapter is designed to help you do the best research possible. First, you get your head around how you intend to use your drone. It's not as cut and dried as you may think. If you plan to use your drone for aerial photography and videography, for example, you need to know the kind of photography or videography you intend to do. You may be taking wedding videos, home tours, pictures of your house, or home movies. This will impact your decision making process greatly!

Next, this chapter also helps you know what to look for before you physically start shopping. You get a good understanding of the types of features you should be looking for and comparing. This chapter cuts through the technical mumbo jumbo so that you understand, specifically, what you should care about and why.

Last, this chapter shows you how to use community reviews and customer feedback to finalize your decision. This chapter will frustrate you if you are an impulsive shopper — or this could be your first step to recovery.

Knowing Where to Start

Buying has gotten a lot easier these days thanks to the Internet. Buying has also gotten a lot harder these days because of the Internet. Not only do you have limitless options on products and product variations, you also have limitless information about each product, its features and the value of the features, and feedback from purchasers (qualified and unqualified). Buying a drone is an exciting endeavor because they are so incredibly cool! But you need to have a method to your shopping, or it will become shopping madness. If money is no object, disregard that statement and just read-aim- BUY! I'm guessing, however, that you want to buy one drone (for now).

But you don't want to buy just any drone. . .

You want to buy the right drone.

To be sure you buy the right drone, you need to take a methodical approach to your shopping. First, know how you will use your drone, and second, get to know the features available on the drones you're considering.

How will you use your drone?

Before you buy a drone, you need to know how you will use it. The reason for this is simple: Every drone has its own set of features and options, some better-suited for certain applications than others. If you plan to use your drone strictly for hobby flying, you want to look for a drone with a built-in camera or no camera at all. Conversely, if you want to use your drone to take pictures and video, you want to look for a drone that comes with a high-quality camera or a mount for your own camera. Whatever scenario you can think of, the important thing to understand is that the way you intend to use your drone should determine which drone you buy.

Here are some questions and explanations to help you think through how you intend to use your drone.

- *Do you intend to fly for hobby purposes only?*

    If you intend to fly your drone for hobby purposes only, you may not need camera support, internal or add-on.

- *Do you intend to fly for extended periods of time?*

    If you intend to fly for extended periods of time, you want to make sure that you have the right balance of motor power and battery life. You also want to consider whether you need the ability to swap out batteries or add additional batteries.

✔ *How do you want to fly? Do you want to fly fast in a straight line?*

If you want to fly fast in a straight line, an airplane or other fixed wing drone may be the right fit. If you want to be able to hover, vertically take off and land, and go in any direction what-so-ever, then a multi-copter may be a good option for you.

✔ *Do you intend to use your drone for aerial pictures or video?*

If you intend to use your drone for aerial pictures or video, you may want to consider camera support. This opens up a litany of additional questions.

✔ *How important are picture and video quality?*

If picture or video quality is of high importance, you may need to consider a drone that can support an add-on camera device.

✔ *How important is streaming video support?*

If streaming video support is of high importance, you need to select a drone with a built-in camera that supports video streaming, or you need to be prepared to make an add-on camera purchase that supports this functionality.

✔ *How far do you want to be able to fly your drone?*

Communication with your controls is a big deal, so you will want to make sure you look at communication methods and distance.

Of course, the age old question that must always be answered is: "What is your budget?" It almost always comes down to this, right? The spectrum of drone pricing is vast. You can spend as little as $100 for a drone and as much as hundreds of thousands of dollars (although pricing in this range is for drones that are intended for more than hobby, personal or small business uses). Establishing a budget can help you whittle down your options.

When contemplating budget, take into consideration how much money you can spend on replacement parts and repairs. It doesn't take much to render a propeller unusable. One serious crash and, depending on the drone, you may have a pricy replacement on your hands.

Whether you are a hobby flyer, photographer, videographer, or maybe you have a use within your business, diving deep into how you intend to use your drone will help you select the right drone.

Drone features

Each drone comes with its own design and feature set. You'll find a direct correlation between price and feature availability. If you want a ton of features, you have pay for them. The first feature you need to pay attention to is the fly package. Most drone manufacturers will make their drones available in either of these packages:

- ✔ **Ready to fly:** A ready-to-fly drone is a drone that comes complete with everything you need to fly. Typically, you need to do some assembly, but this is typically limited to attaching propellers and plugging in batteries.

- ✔ **Bind and fly:** More advanced drone flyers may have their own remote controllers or maybe even a high-end or custom built ground-control system. For this reason, some drones are available as a drone-only package. *Bind and fly* simply means you need to bind your drone to your controller before you can start flying.

Understanding the difference between these two packages will save you some headaches and also help you if you are budgeting to purchase a drone. First-time drone-buyers will always want to buy a ready to fly because it comes with everything needed to get up and running right away! Other features that your drone might offer beyond a different paint job include:

- ✔ **Advanced control options:** Different communication protocols, such as Bluetooth or Wi-Fi, enable you to connect your drone to a computer, smartphone, or tablet.

- ✔ **GPS home function:** Drones with this function know where they started flying from and attempt to return to that location if there is a problem. (This is not something you should rely on.)

- ✔ **GPS navigation:** GPS navigation makes it possible to track your drone or program routes.

- ✔ **Streaming video:** Drones with this capability let you stream video from a first person video view or simply stream video back to a computer, phone, or tablet.

- ✔ **Power:** Payload size, battery life, and propeller speeds all impact flight time, flight radius, and so on.

- ✔ **Camera support:** Built-in (*integrated*) cameras and add-on camera support give you flexibility in how you use your drone for video and photography.

Drones with Integrated Cameras

If you're looking into buying a drone because you are interested in aerial photography or videography, your first major decision will be whether or not to purchase a drone that comes with a built-in camera or simply supports an add-on camera. As with anything, there are pros and cons to purchasing a drone with built-in camera support. Drones with add-on cameras are covering later in this chapter, in the section, "Drones with Add-On Camera Support."

The pros for purchasing a drone with an integrated camera include:

- **Ease of use:** A drone with a built-in camera does not require much setup or configuring beyond charging batteries and plugging in a storage device like a USB drive or SD card.

- **Flight-specific filming features:** Drones with integrated cameras typically have advanced features like video streaming to mobile devices and recording to remote storage. This is very helpful for viewing what you're shooting as you shoot it. Also, you can record the streaming video footage to remote storage so you can back up the footage as you film it to protect against failures on your storage media.

- **Support:** Support for your drone means support for your camera. This may seem like a small thing, but it's one less call and one less warranty you have to deal with.

The cons of purchasing a drone with an integrated camera include:

- **Camera quality:** Drone companies build drones, not cameras. Therefore, integrated cameras are typically an afterthought and lack the power of an add-on camera of a reputable brand.

- **Custom features:** Integrated cameras tend to lack custom features and controls that are typical of an add-on camera, such as manual image adjustment modes, recording modes, and frame rates.

- **Battery life:** Integrated cameras typically feed off of the main battery. Adding additional batteries will add additional weight and thus reduce fly times.

Integrated camera features

When making a decision on a drone with an integrated camera, there will be several different features that you should take into consideration. These features include:

- **Sensor size:** Digital cameras have an internal sensor that captures light information and then translates that information into data to make your picture file. As it goes, the bigger the sensor, the better the image because the more light it can gather. Small cameras will always have small censors. Figure 2-1 shows a diagram comparing sensor sizes of various cameras.

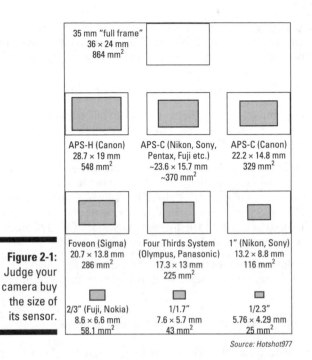

Figure 2-1: Judge your camera buy the size of its sensor.

35 mm "full frame"
36 × 24 mm
864 mm^2

APS-H (Canon)
28.7 × 19 mm
548 mm^2

APS-C (Nikon, Sony, Pentax, Fuji etc.)
~23.6 × 15.7 mm
~370 mm^2

APS-C (Canon)
22.2 × 14.8 mm
329 mm^2

Foveon (Sigma)
20.7 × 13.8 mm
286 mm^2

Four Thirds System
(Olympus, Panasonic)
17.3 × 13 mm
225 mm^2

1" (Nikon, Sony)
13.2 × 8.8 mm
116 mm^2

2/3" (Fuji, Nokia)
8.6 × 6.6 mm
58.1 mm^2

1/1.7"
7.6 × 5.7 mm
43 mm^2

1/2.3"
5.76 × 4.29 mm
25 mm^2

Source: Hotshot977

✔ **Lens:** The camera lens is almost as important as the sensor size. This is because the lens is responsible for focusing and directing light into the sensor. The size and shape of the lens will greatly affect image quality, almost as much as the sensor size.

✔ **Resolution:** In video, the *resolution* is the number of dots (pixels) that can be squeezed into the video image. You might think of resolution in terms of your television because the quality of your television is typically measured by its resolution. A television that is high definition has a resolution of at least 1280x720. That means 720 pixels vertically and 1280 pixels horizontally make up the image on the screen. Sample high-definition resolutions include 720i, 720p, 1080i, 1080p. Ultra definition is an image that is bigger than 1080p.

✔ **Frame rate:** The number of times a camera can take a picture in a second is *frame rate*. The most common frame rate for film is 24 frames per second. Higher frame rates are useful in improving the look of video in high and ultra-definition. Higher frame rates can also be slowed down to create slow motion.

✔ **Photo resolution:** *Photo resolution,* which is measured in megapixels, is a misleading number because the quality of an image has more to do with the size and quality of the pixel not the number of the pixels.

✔ **File format:** Digital images and video are stored in files, which are save in different *file formats*. Different file formats require different software to open and manipulate them. Different digital image and video files also have different levels of compression. *Compression* removes information from a file to make the file size smaller. In images and video, compression means a loss of quality.

✔ **Storage options:** Integrated cameras may come with the option to add external storage like a USB drive or an SD card for storing pictures and video. The more the storage, the fewer the times you'll need to swap media or dump footage which equals longer flying times. Figure 2-2 shows a USB storage device, SD card, and MicroSD card.

Figure 2-2: Compares different drone storage media.

Courtesy of Tucker Krajewski

Buying a drone that has an integrated camera

There are currently several drones available for purchase that come equipped with an integrated camera. Each drone comes with a unique mixture of features and quality. Take a look at the features of the drones described in the following sections.

DJI Phantom 2 Vision

The DJI Phantom 2 Vision is shown in Figure 2-3. It includes the following features:

- ✔ **14 megapixel camera**
- ✔ **Resolution/Frame Rates:** 1080/30p or 1080/60i
- ✔ **Sensor Size:** 1/2.3 inches (Super small)
- ✔ **Storage:** MicroSD Card (32GB Limit)
- ✔ **Lens:** 100°

Parrot AR Drone 2.0

The Parrot AR Drone 2.0 is shown in Figure 2-4. It includes the following features:

- ✔ **Video Resolution/Frame Rate:** 720p
- ✔ **Lens:** 92°
- ✔ **Storage:** USB or stream
- ✔ **Video Format:** H.264

Figure 2-3:
DJI
Phantom 2
Vision with
camera.

Source: WalterPro4755/Creative Commons

Figure 2-4:
Parrot
AR Drone
2.0 with
camera.

Source: Christopher Michel/Creative Commons

Drones with Add-On Camera Support

Buying a drone that comes with support to add your own camera is a great option for photographers and videographers that have a greater concern for the quality of the images and video they intend to capture. Of course, this option does come with its own bag of goodies and bummers.

The pros to purchasing a drone with add-on camera support include:

- **Camera options:** With this sort of drone, you can control what camera you fly. If you want to fly an action camera, cinema camera, or DSLR, the only thing standing in your way is your drone's payload limitation.

- **Battery life:** Your camera runs on its own battery which means that constant video or photo usage will not impact your drone's battery life.

- **Total control:** With picking your own camera, you can control the way you capture footage, the format of your footage, and the way your footage is stored. You also get more options for how you stabilize your camera with additional mounting hardware like Gimbals (more on these in Chapter 14).

The cons to purchasing a drone with add-on camera support include:

- ✔ **Weight:** Depending on the camera and lens that you use, your rig could get extremely heavy pretty quickly. Flying a heavier rig will require a more powerful rig, which doesn't come cheaply.

- ✔ **Finesse features:** Drones with integrated cameras usually come with slick features like streaming video to an iPhone or tablet, remote video and camera controls, and remote streaming recording. These features are possible with third party cameras and hardware, but the features won't be integrated into your drone's flight software, which means you may need some extra hands.

- ✔ **Technical support:** When you crash your drone, you'll need to call your drone manufacturer for concerns relating to your drone. You'll need to contact your camera manufacturer separately to get repairs, address warranty issues, and other things along those lines.

- ✔ **Price:** If you don't already have your camera equipment, you'll need to purchase the camera equipment and that can drastically inflate your costs to get up and running. Not to mention, accessories don't come cheaply, either.

There are several types of cameras on the market that will work wonderfully with your new drone. The question is whether you should pick your camera first and then select your drone or if you should pick your drone before you pick your camera. The good news is that there is a drone for pretty much any camera out there. Just remember, the bigger the gear, the bigger the drone, and the bigger the drone, the bigger the price tag.

Action cameras

Action cameras live up to their name because they are designed specifically to capture traditional and extreme sports. Action cameras typically capture video footage at extremely high frame rates making the fast movements look smooth at normal speeds or in slow motion. Action cameras are also very durable and designed to be in extreme situations like under water, strapped to a sky diver, or affixed to the end of a snow ski or the end of a surf board.

Not only do action cameras gather high-quality footage in extreme situations, they are also extremely compact which makes them ideal for pairing with a drone. There are several action cameras available to consumers but the GoPro brand of cameras has solidified themselves as the industry leader. GoPro is so pervasive in action cameras that the name is used almost interchangeable with action camera, similar to how you might ask for a Kleenex when you need a Kleenex . . . I mean tissue.

Other players, if you want to call them that, in the GoPro market, I mean action camera market, include Sony, JVC, and Garmin, but none of them even remotely compares to the GoPro. Figure 2-5 shows two types of action cameras.

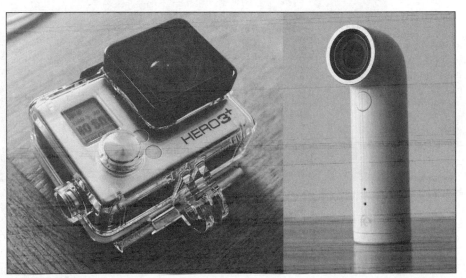

Figure 2-5:
Two types
of action
cameras.

Source: Andreas Kambanis/Creative Commons
Source: TechStage/Creative Commons

Point-and-shoot/compact cameras

The term *point-and-shoot* is primarily used to describe small compact digital cameras designed for inexperienced photographers. They make taking good photos and video easier by providing, almost exclusively, auto features like auto light adjustment, auto color adjustment, auto focus, and auto zoom. Small point & shoot cameras can be as small as a small stack of credit cards. Bigger point-and-shoot cameras are available, however, that offer additional features such as manual controls, interchangeable lenses, and lens attachments, to name a few.

Point-and-shoot cameras also offer the user an affordable way into the world of video. Most point-and-shoot cameras come equipped with a video feature. This is handy if you are a budding videographer because you can check out video without needing to make much of a financial commitment. One thing to keep in mind is that point-and-shoot cameras are designed for ease of use and low cost. The quality of the pictures and video is fantastic given the price and available controls and features, but these are not intended to satisfy the desires of the more experienced photographer. Figure 2-6 is a picture of several different small to mid-sized point-and-shoot cameras.

Figure 2-6: Point-and-shoot cameras are cute.

DSLR cameras

DSLR stands for digital single-lens reflex. There are several types of DSLR cameras on the market and they all range in size and price. DSLR cameras are wonderful for capturing stunning images because they have large image sensors, interchangeable lenses, several file storage modes, and depending on your camera, a whole slew of manual control features.

Most of the major electronics manufacturers have a line of DSLR cameras ranging in size, features, and price. Depending on who you ask, you will get varying opinions on what equipment package is the best. If you don't already have a DSLR, be prepared for option overload! However, you can always focus on the big two: Nikon and Canon. Just looking into those two brands will keep you busy for months as you navigate their robust offerings of cameras.

Using a DSLR camera with a drone is going to present several obstacles to overcome with the main one being price. DSLR cameras, lenses, and other accessories are expensive. They are also heavy which means that you will need a drone powerful enough to be able to not only lift your gear, but have enough power and battery to be able to sustain fly times that will be worthwhile. Figure 2-7 is a picture of popular Canon and Nikon DSLR cameras as well as several lenses.

Courtesy of Tucker Krajewski

Figure 2-7:
DSLR
cameras
and lenses.

Cinema-quality cameras

If you are serious about video, you may be thinking about using a cinema-quality camera. There are several high-quality digital cameras that can be used to capture insanely good video footage without totally breaking the bank. The reason why I refer to them as cinema-quality is because they capture that caliber of footage but won't require you to put a fourth mortgage on your home in order to buy them. These cameras produce outstanding footage, but weight is an issue.

One very popular cinema-quality camera is the Black Magic Pocket Cinema Camera. This camera is compact, and it supports popular DSLR lenses as well as higher-end cinema style lenses. Lenses are funny because the bigger and heavier they are, the more they cost. They feel expensive!

Another powerful cinema-quality camera is the Canon C-series of cameras. This series of cameras is built specifically for video. They support Canon DSLR lenses, and their quality far surpasses action cameras, DSLR cameras, and other consumer grade video cameras. Figure 2-8 is a picture of the Black Magic and Canon C1-series cameras.

Figure 2-8: Popular cinema-quality cameras.

Courtesy of Tucker Krajewski

Flight Controls

Drones can't just fly themselves. Well, actually, they can. But the whole point of flying your drone is actually flying it! Controlling a drone can happen in a number of ways. First and foremost, you must understand how flight controls work. At the basic level, your drone is equipped with a receiver. The receiver receives information that tells it what to do. You tell your drone what to do using a transmitter. Since the dawn of remote control flight, receivers and transmitters have communicated using radio frequencies (RF).

Not much has changed with remote controls. What has changed, is the numerous additional communication methods built into consumer drones today:

✔ GPS provides accurate position data for your drone. It also allows for some pretty slick auto pilot features.

✔ Wi-Fi provides the ability to transmit heavy amounts of data to and from the drone within a specific control radius.

✔ Bluetooth provides another method for transmitting information to and from the drone.

✔ 900Mhz/433Mhz provides longer range communication at a slower data rate.

The additional communication methods have opened the door to some pretty awesome drone flying features. Some drones have thrown out remote control with handheld transmitters and replaced them with smartphone and tablet controls. Flight controls are a major differentiator between drones and a very important feature to take into consideration when choosing a drone!

RC Transmitters

Most drones come with an RC transmitter. RC controls are very basic and typically only offer directional control. RC transmitters provide control of your drone for a much greater distance than a Wi-Fi or Bluetooth connection. Most drones will come with an RC transmitter designed specifically for them, although RC transmitters can be interchangeable, so you can use a third party RC transmitter if you want. If you are going to use a third-party RC transmitter, make sure you verify that it is compatible with your drone or the matching receiver can be installed in your drone.

Your drone should come with documentation to specify which transmitters are compatible with it. If you can't find the information in your operating manual or online, then you may want to hold off on purchasing a transmitter. An incompatible transmitter will only be useful as a paper weight, or contemporary art. Figure 2-9 shows several RC Transmitters that are used with all sorts of drones.

Drones are typically offered in two different package types: ready-to-fly means all you need to fly are included in the box and there is next to no assembly required; bind-and-fly means you need to set your drone up to work with your own remote control handset.

Figure 2-9:
Several RC transmitters.

Courtesy of Tucker Krajewski

Mobile Apps

Wi-Fi and Bluetooth have made it possible for drone manufacturers to create device controls that run on smartphone or tablet. Not just a smartphone version of your RC transmitter, but high-tech controls. Several drone manufactures have created apps that give you advanced positioning, first person video controls, programmable flight routes, and more.

Some drones come with both an RC transmitter controller and a mobile application for viewing you're the drone's position using GPS, flight stats like speed, battery life, and fly time. Figure 2-10 is a picture of a drone control app.

Figure 2-10: A sample drone control applications.

Courtesy of Tucker Krajewski

Advanced flight modes

Drone manufacturers have come up with several useful flight modes and autopilots to make flying with a purpose a little bit easier. Advanced flight modes can also help you recover a drone that has gone rogue.

✔ **Set it and forget it:** Program a flight path for your drone into a mobile or tablet app and then watch it go. (Be careful where you tell your drone to fly – drones go exactly where you tell them to go, even if a building is in the way!)

✔ **Auto return home:** GPS locking your drone before you start flying will make it possible for your drone to return home if it loses data connection or flies out of range of your controller.

✔ **Follow mode:** Using an app or other controller makes it possible for your drone to follow you at a specified altitude and distance.

Batteries

Consumer drones run on electricity, unlike their big brothers in the military that use some form of a combustion engine (or solar). Your drone must have a reliable power source, and that means batteries. The problem with batteries is that they are heavy, must be charged, and they are typically expensive. And remember, batteries on motorized vehicles typically don't last long. When selecting a drone, take the following criteria into consideration:

- ✔ **Battery composition:** Drones should be powered with LiPo batteries. LiPo batteries are much better than their NiCad older brothers because they output power faster, store larger amounts of power, and have a longer life.

- ✔ **Battery life:** How long will the drone battery last under normal usage? The bigger the drone, the bigger the battery you will need. Under normal usage (meaning not a lot of wind or cold weather), your drone should be able to fly at least 15 minutes. More than that is a big win.

- ✔ **Proprietary technology:** Does the drone require you to use the manufacturer's specific battery? Requiring you to use a specific battery with a proprietary connector is one way manufacturers can make extra cash. Figure 2-11 shows some aftermarket batteries and proprietary batteries for the DJI Phantom drone series. Having the option of using an aftermarket battery may save you money in the long run.

- ✔ **Replacement cost:** Consider the cost of spare or replacement batteries. For example, the DJI Phantom 2 is a $500 drone. A replacement battery for the DJI Phantom 2 battery is around $100. That means that batteries are 20 percent of the cost of this particular drone. The 3D robotics Iris+ is around $750 and the cost of a replacement battery is $40 which means that the battery is roughly 5 percent of the cost.

- ✔ **Charging:** Does your drone come with a charging station? Charging stations aren't as expensive as the batteries but every little accessory can add up. Charge times tend to be relative to the capacity of the battery. You can shorten charge time by using a charger with a higher output, which is indicated by amps. For example, the DJI Phantom 2 charger is 2 amps and it will take an hour to an hour and a half to charge the battery. Using an aftermarket charger that charges at 6 amps would cut down the charge time by over half. Proceed with caution when charging your drone battery. Chapter 6 gets into the danger of LiPo batteries.

Your drone's total weight, power of the motors, and size of the propellers will all play a role in determining how long your drone can stay airborne. The battery, however, will ultimately decide your flying time. Without power, nothing else matters! Most drones come with an average flight time rating. This rating is based off average use in reasonable weather conditions.

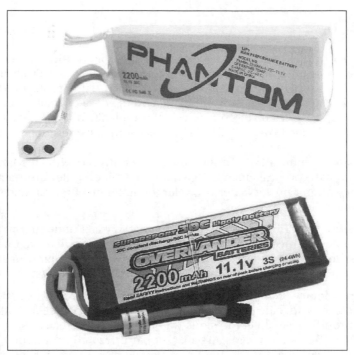

Courtesy of Mark LaFay

Other Important Features

Drones have several other features that are worth looking into and comparing, but they are on the more technical side of things and somewhat out of
scope of this book. They are, however, worth mentioning so that you can
choose to do research on them if you are so inclined.

- ✔ **Composition:** Drones are made from materials such as plastic, carbon
  fiber, metal, and Styrofoam. Each material has benefits. For instance,
  plastic is inexpensive but not very durable. Carbon fiber is durable and
  light but expensive. Styrofoam is light and cheaper than plastic but not
  the most durable. At some point, when you crash your drone, the material
  that comprise your drone will largely determine how likely your drone
  is to survive. Although nothing is indestructible and at some point, all
  materials will fail.

- ✔ **Payload capacity:** *Payload capacity* is a feature that is important for photographers and videographers. If you choose to use a high-end camera
  such as a DSLR or cinema-quality camera, you will need to know how
  much weight your drone can lift and how it will affect your fly times.

Where to Buy Your Drone

When you're ready to buy a drone, your best option is to purchase online. Most manufacturers sell direct to consumer so your best bet may be to go directly to a manufacturer's website. The other obvious answer when buying online is to go to Amazon or other massive e-retailers to see what sort of drone options you have. The technology is still quite new so there are only a handful of manufacturers that have grown large enough to be able to support a widespread distribution partnership with a retailer like Amazon. Therefore, the selection of drones on Amazon won't represent the majority of your options.

The drone industry has been growing at a rapid pace and as a result, several new companies have been springing up overnight. Some drone companies are privately funded while others like Airdroids, Hexo+, and Airdox were funded using crowdfunding sites like Kickstarter and Indiegogo.

These smaller companies are building great products with truly unique features, but the demand is so great that it's difficult to keep up and therefore major distribution deals are not only not needed yet, they are unmanageable. Your best bet is to go to their company websites and buy directly.

Another option for locating the drone that is perfect for you is from photography and video equipment retailers. Companies like B&H or Adorama are major online and physical retailers of drones and drone accessories.

TIP

Using customer reviews

One of the major benefits to shopping for drones online with sites like Amazon, B&H, and Adorama is the collection of customer feedback on the products. To further qualify community feedback, Amazon recently started publicly indicating whether or not feedback was coming from someone that purchased the product being reviewed. Amazon community feedback can now also contain pictures and images. This feedback can be wildly helpful for making a decision regardless of whether you decide to buy on Amazon.

If you don't trust online feedback, your other option is to get plugged into a local drone hobby group. The benefit to participating in these groups before you own a drone is that you can learn from users, and you can probably try before you buy. You will learn more about getting social with drones in Chapter 4.

Chapter 3

Picking the Best Camera for Your Needs

In This Chapter

▶ Knowing your camera's intended use

▶ Determining how much weight your drone supports

▶ Choosing a digital camera

▶ Comparing features and price

As you search for your perfect drone, you will quickly see that there is an increasingly vast array of options. You want to consider the drone's power and the distance it will fly before its battery requires recharging. You want to research its controls, look, and feel. And if you decide to purchase a drone that does not come with an integrated camera, you will have to make another difficult decision: what type of camera will you purchase?

This chapter helps you make an informed choice of camera and camera accessories. It's okay if you haven't decided whether to purchase a drone with or without a camera. This chapter will likely push you over to one side of the fence.

In this chapter, you navigate a number of uses for your aerial camera rig specifically to help you narrow down how you most commonly intend to use your drone and associated camera. You see the major differences between DSLR cameras and action cameras before diving deep into the nitty-gritty features that make each camera type suited for a specific use. Then you explore the capabilities of each camera category by looking at their features and how those features will help you achieve different results.

Last, and definitely not least if you are cost conscious at all, this chapter will be beneficial to you in that it will help you identify a camera that has the right amount of power and features at the right price. Purchasing your drone and camera is an investment no matter how you slice it. You are either investing in a creative outlet or you are investing in your business. Making the right purchase will maximize the benefit you receive.

Knowing How You Will Use Your Camera

Cameras that have many features and capabilities can cost more, even much more, than their simpler counterparts. While money may not be an initial driver in your decision-making process, you will find that cost can, and will, spiral out of control very quickly. Your best bet is to identify a camera that neither exceeds nor falls short of your needs. To find an ideal match, you must assess how you will use the camera with your drone.

To help determine how you intend to use your camera, consider the following:

✔ *Determine whether you will be using your aerial photo/video rig primarily for hobby, or if you will be using it professionally.*

Hobby uses and professional uses can look identical depending on how seriously you take your hobbies. A personal assessment of need versus want combined with disposable income will help you make a decision on the level of features and investment you should make in your camera gear. Determining this balance is difficult for hobbyists because the decision is far more emotional than it is mathematical. Selecting gear for a professional application is a little easier because you can strip away the emotion to make a decision that is driven by dollars and sense.

✔ *Determine whether your core use is for photography or video.*

Most digital cameras that are designed for photography can capture video, and many of the digital video cameras have the option to capture stills. That said, if you want to take spectacular photos, you need to focus on cameras that can capture great photos. If you have some video needs, then a camera with video capabilities as a secondary feature may suffice. The same goes for video. If your primary use will be to capture video footage, focus on a camera designed for video. Pulling still photos from video footage isn't ideal because it is tedious, but it is possible. Some video devices may also have photo capabilities as well.

✔ *Consider where your video or photography will be used.*

How will your finished work be used? Will you be printing photos in publications or to be framed and hung on the wall at home? Are you making videos to play on your smartphone or will it be for your ultra-high-definition television at home?

✔ *Where and when will you capture the majority of the footage?*

If you plan to capture videos and photos outside, then you need to decide whether or not you will be working in the elements. Will you have to work in the rain or snow, extreme temperatures, sandy or dusty air? If so, you will need to look for a camera that has options for handling these environments. If you plan to work with low-light much, you will want to ensure that the camera you choose works well in low light.

Determining What Your Drone Supports

If you haven't purchased your drone, then the best place to start looking is on the drone manufacturer's website. Identify which drone you are interested in and then navigate to the product specifications list. This should include information on the type of camera or cameras the device supports. Most drone manufacturers are quite explicit on the type of camera they support. However, if you cannot find any information online, you should look to see if the drone supports a gimbal. *Gimbals* are special camera mounts that can provide a range of features, such as image stabilization and camera directional control. Gimbals are typically made for a specific type of camera. Therefore, knowing what gimbal your drone supports will help you narrow down to the types of cameras you can use.

If you are selecting a camera based on the type of mounts that will work with your drone, you need to make sure that your gimbal and camera will not exceed the drone's payload maximum. This number is typically listed on the drone's product spec page on the manufacturer's website. It will be listed either as payload capacity or take-off weight. For more information on the importance of minding the weight of your camera and mounting equipment, see the next section, "Weight Is Everything."

If you have already purchased a drone, then you should refer to your drone's owner's manual. The manual contains information on the type of camera your drone supports along with how to attach it to your drone. If you're like my friend Colleen, chances are good that you will lose your owner's manual. The good news is that most popular drone companies like DJI, Parrot, or 3D Robotics have online versions!

Weight Is Everything

There is a direct correlation between size of the camera and total price of your aerial imaging gear. The reason for this is that the bigger cameras require more robust mounting equipment and all the extra weight means that the drone needs to be more powerful to be able to get it off the ground. Like all aircraft, drones are a careful balance of propeller size, motor strength, battery power, and total weight.

Lift is what causes heavier-than-air objects to become airborne. Planes achieve lift by moving air over their wings. Rotor-craft, like drones, create lift by moving air over their propellers.

The heavier the aircraft, the more air that must be moved to achieve weightlessness. Figure 3-1 shows a heavy duty drone and camera rig.

You can do this by merely spinning your propellers faster, but propellers can only go so fast before centrifugal force causes them to become turbulent and unstable. The other option is to just use larger propellers so that you displace more air per revolution. Larger propellers, however, are heavier and with the increased surface area, increased resistance occurs, which means you need a more powerful motor. When you add a more powerful motor, you have an increase of total weight from the motor and rotor and you have an increase in power consumption. More power consumption means that you will need a more powerful battery and as batteries go up in output and capacity, they go up in total weight. Larger propellers also require greater clearance between each other.

Figure 3-1:
A massive
drone and
camera rig.

Source: European Southern Observatory (ESO)/ Creative Commons.

Because of these factors, you will typically see larger and heavier camera equipment supported by drones with six to eight rotor/propellers, like the one shown in Figure 3-2, which shows an octocopter (8 rotors). More propellers means more air displacement which equates to a greater lift capacity. As you can tell by Figure 3-2, these craft are quite a bit bigger than the tri and quad copters that support smaller action cameras.

Figure 3-2:
Octocopters
have
8 propellers.

Source: Service-drone.com

Digital Camera Technology

Camera technology has come a long way in the past 25 years. So far, in fact, that film photography has become something reserved for film purists and nostalgia. Some would argue that film is still far superior to digital photo much in the way that music purists argue that records are far superior to digital media. In a way they are probably right, but it really is hard to tell the difference these days because digital technology has advanced so far.

Film cameras and digital cameras function in a very similar manner. When taking a picture with a film camera, a shutter opens for a brief moment to allow in light. The light is then focused and reflected onto a piece of film. The film captures the image exactly as it was seen through the lens of the camera. When a roll of film is developed, the film is chemically treated so that it is no longer reactive to light. The end result is a *negative,* a transparent piece of plastic that contains your image. Shine a light on your negative to project an image onto a screen or onto a piece of paper to make a photo.

Digital cameras function much in the same manner. A shutter opens to allow in light through the lens. The light is then focused and reflected onto a sensor instead of a piece of film. The sensor then translates the light information into pixels, which are organized and stored in a digital file. Digital video works much in the same manner as digital photography.

With so many digital cameras available, you have many features to choose from. If you are interested in learning about those features in depth, see *Digital SLR Cameras and Photography For Dummies* (Wiley).

Aside from price, here are the primary features that require consideration when selecting your new camera:

- ✔ **Sensor size and type:** Digital camera sensors capture the image information and convert it into a digital image. The two primary sensors that are widely used today are CMOS and CCD sensors. There is some debate over which sensor type is the better option, but really, sensor size is the more important consideration. The larger the sensor means the greater the image information that can be captured. Figure 3-3 shows a digital camera sensor.

- ✔ **Lens:** Your camera lens gathers and focuses the light that makes up your picture. Several types of lenses are available that create different effects. Maybe you want a close-up shot that is very focused, or maybe you want a distant that is clear as can be. Different lenses serve these different purposes. Having the option to change out your lenses to perform different functions is a huge plus for professional photographers and videographers. Integrated lenses are cheaper and they are typically designed to work in numerous scenarios; however, the saying goes "A jack of all trades is a master of none," and the same goes for integrated lenses. Figure 3-4 shows several types of lenses.

- ✔ **Image processor (file types):** Once an image is captured by the sensor, it must be converted into a digital file. Your camera's *image processor* compresses the image into a variety of different file types. Keep in mind that the term *compress* is synonymous with "throwing away potentially useful image information for the sake of saving space." Shooting in RAW is the only way to not lose image information. *RAW* is essentially everything that your image sensor detects. RAW files take up a lot of space, about two to three times more than a comparable JPEG, which is why an image processor is valuable. Compression also means that you need fewer SD cards for storing your images.

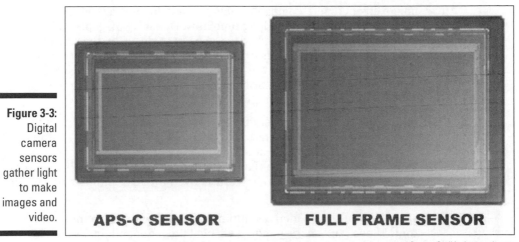

Figure 3-3:
Digital camera sensors gather light to make images and video.

Source: Onslidephotography.com

Figure 3-4:
Lenses small and large serve a number of purposes.

Source: mecookie/Creative Commons

✔ **Image size:** Camera companies have been using megapixel ratings as a marketing gimmick for a long time now. Debating megapixels is like debating Nikon and Canon. Pixels are used to describe the size of an image, not the overall quality of the image. More megapixels means the bigger your prints can be. Thanks to today's technology, we can make an 80-foot-by-20-foot print of my mother. Bottom-line, the larger the megapixel rating, the better.

✔ **Video options:** Every camera today should come with the option to capture video. DSLR cameras and point-and-shoot cameras, for the most part, have a video mode that allows you to capture video footage. You may want to pick a camera that has video capability, whether you think you'll use it or not. It's a great feature, even if you don't intend to use it frequently.

✔ **Video resolutions:** Video resolution has to do with the number of horizontal lines (and corresponding vertical lines depending on the video's formatted aspect ratio). For instance, if you are viewing something in full high-definition, then you are viewing an image that is made up with 1080 horizontal lines of picture information. The higher the definition, the crisper and more vibrant the image should appear on your display device. If you are interested in video, you want to make sure that the video capabilities of your camera are at minimum HD. Some cameras will capture ultra-high-definition, which means higher than HD. 2k is essentially 2 times the definition of HD; 4k is 4 times, and so on. Figure 3-5 compares the different video resolutions.

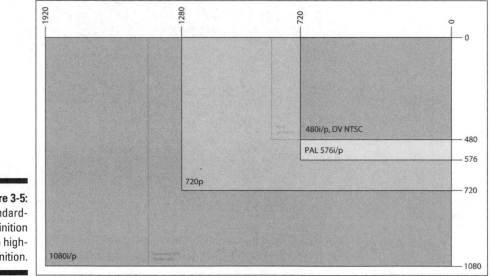

Figure 3-5:
Standard-definition
to high-definition.

Source: en.wikipedia.org/TVaughan1

✔ **Frame rates:** Video is a sequence of photos. There is a lot of debate on how many pictures the human eye and brain can process per second, but the industry standard has been 24.7 frames per second for a long time. That means that in video, you show 24.7 pictures per second to make the video look smooth and buttery. However, cameras today can capture video at higher frame rates which means more pictures per second and ultimately, an even smoother looking video.

An added benefit to higher frame rates is smooth slow motion. If you were to slow down a video shot at 30 frames per second, it would look and feel like a family slide show. However, if you shot a video at 120 frames per second and you slowed it down to 30 frames per second, your video would be silky smooth and it would be moving at one quarter the speed. Imagine the action shots that would look amazing in slow motion!

Picking a point-and-shoot camera

Point-and-shoot cameras are small, easy-to-use digital cameras. The point-and-shoot camera is a great way to get a digital camera at a low price. These cameras were designed to take pictures without much thought (if any at all). They are great for the beginning photographer or the photographer that doesn't really care to take the time to set up a shot. Of course, with automatic settings, you are at the mercy of the intelligence built into the camera.

Point-and-shoot cameras are also designed to be compact so that they can fit in your pocket and be taken virtually anywhere. The smaller size means that their image sensors are extremely small, which will affect the quality of your pictures. That's not to say that you can't take really beautiful pictures with a point-and-shoot camera. These photos will just not be comparable to the images you can take with a full-size DSLR (covered in the next section, "Deciding on a DSLR camera").

Point-and-shoot cameras rarely, if ever, come with support for additional lenses, so you are at the mercy of the integrated lens and zoom. This is great for keeping the overall weight of your camera rig down. However if you want to get different effects that can only be produced by incorporating different lenses, you're out of luck. Most point-and-shoot cameras have a video mode, however, which is great for having the option to capture video on a device that is designed more specifically for capturing fantastic pictures. Several types of drones support point-and-shoot cameras. To get an idea of the different types of point and shoot cameras currently available, take a look at Figure 3-6.

	Panasonic Lumix	Olympus S	Canon PowerShot A	Sony Cyber-Shot W	Fujifilm FinePix F	Olympus V	Fujifilm FinePix T	Samsung Smart ST	Canon PowerShot ELPH	Nikon CoolPix S
Image Quality										
Image Sensor	CCD	CMOS	CCD	CCD	CMOS	CCD	CCD	CCD	CMOS	CCD
Resolution (megapixels)	16.1	16	16	18.2	16	16	16	16.2	16.1	16
Minimum ISO Setting	100	125	100	100	100	100	100	80	100	80
Maximum ISO Setting	3200	6400	3200	3200	12800	1600	3200	3200	3200	3200
Optical Zoom	20X	24X	5X	5X	20X	12X	12X	5X	5X	6X
Digital Zoom	4X	4X	4X	20X	2X	4X	24X	14X	4X	4X
Minimum Shutter Speed (seconds)	1/4,000	1/2,000	1/2,000	1/2,000	1/2,000	1/2,000	1/2,000	1/2,000	1/2,000	1/2,000
Maximum Shutter Speed (seconds)	250	4	1	2	8	4	8	16	1	1
HD Video Quality	720p	1080p	720p	720p	1080p	720p	1080p	720p	720p	720p
Red Eye Reduction	X	X	X	X	X	X	X	X	X	X
White Balance	X	X	X	X	X	X	X	X	X	X
Image Stabilizer	X	X	X	X	X	X	X	X	X	X
Motion Blur Suppression	X	X	X	X	X			X	X	X
Settings & Effects										
Self Timer	X	X	X	X	X	X	X	X	X	X
Color Effects	X	X	X	X	X	X	X	X	X	X
Slideshow	X	X	X	X	X		X	X		X
Panorama	X	X		X	X	X	X	X		X
Face Recognition	X			X					X	X
Wi-Fi Functions	X		X							
Audio Recordings	X	X	X	X		X	X	X	X	
Shadow Adjustment		X				X	X	X		
Photo Touchup	X	X	X	X	X	X	X	X	X	X
Battery Life & Storage										
Battery Life (shots per charge)	260	310	200	240	300	220	200	N/A	170	180
Internal Memory (MB)	90	39.9	74	19	21	34.9	None	10	None	42
Expandable Memory	X	X	X	X	X	X	X	X	X	X
Li-ion Rechargeable Battery	X	X	X	X	X	X	X	X	X	X
Design										
Display Screen Size (inches)	3	3	2.7	2.7	3	3	3	3	3	2.7
Width (inches)	4.13	4.4	3.73	3.75	4.1	3.8	3.9	3.67	3.67	3.8
Height (inches)	2.27	2.5	2.43	2.13	2.4	2.2	2.2	2.11	2.24	2.4
Depth (inches)	1.31	1.6	1.17	0.78	1.4	0.8	1	0.67	0.79	0.9
Weight (ounces)	7.73	9.5	6.14	4.7	8.1	4.4	4.9	3.9	4.76	5
Touch Screen	x	x	x	x	x	x	x	x	x	x

Figure 3-6: Compare and contrast point-and-shoot cameras.

Point and shoot cameras are great for capturing good quality pictures without spending too much time configuring a camera. These cameras typically come with great automatic settings that can adapt to their environment on the fly. These cameras are also light which makes them a great option for smaller drones. Point and shoot cameras are also a little more durable than their DSLR big brothers. This is a great feature when strapping them to a flying computer that could potentially fly through a waterfall, crash into a tree, or fall out of the sky. Lastly, you can't really argue with the price. Point-and-shoot cameras are in a price range that is affordable for many!

Deciding on a DSLR camera

DSLR stands for *digital single light reflex,* and the term is used to categorize high-end consumer and professional quality digital cameras. DSLR cameras come with a huge range of features and technical capabilities, which is why their uses span from hobby to professional. DSLR cameras have larger sensors than their point-and-shoot little brothers. Bigger is definitely more expensive when it comes to DSLRs. Bigger sensors come at a high price point, but they also provide much better imaging capabilities.

DSLR cameras can be for the beginning and aspiring photographer. Smaller cameras still come with several manual Image control features and the option to swap out images. This gives the user the ability to try different combinations of settings and lenses. DSLR cameras are much larger and heavier than point-and-shoot cameras. They are also a little more complex, which may slow you down when you are setting up your drone. Figure 3-7 shows a few different DSLR cameras with lenses.

While DSLR cameras were original developed purely for photography, in recent years, DSLR manufacturers started adding in video modes. This was intended to give users the option to capture some footage, but it was never intended to be the sole purpose of the camera. DSLR video footage can look so incredible, however, that video geeks everywhere have started using DSLR cameras specifically for video.

Here are just a few reasons why DSLR cameras are an appealing choice for recording video footage:

- **Price point:** The price point for a DSLR is much lower than video cameras of comparable quality
- **Lenses:** Seemingly infinite options are available for lenses
- **File storage:** The DSLR cameras store video footage in file format on SD cards instead of tape or the more expensive P2 cards seen in high-end pro cameras

Figure 3-8 is a picture of a video rig using a DSLR camera.

Figure 3-7:
A DSLR
for every
occasion.

Figure 3-8:
DSLR
video rig.

One major problem with filming on DSLR is that big image sensors get extremely hot when used in video mode. DSLR cameras did not come with any sort of cooling built into the cameras, which means that overheating is a major issue. To work around this, you can capture video short chunks before having to shut down the camera and restart it.

DSLR cameras are a great camera for people who are serious about photography and video. The major drawback is that DSLRs are heavier than the point-and-shoot cameras, and depending on the lens, weight and balance can become a major issue. Remember, the heavier it is, the more it is going to cost you! You are going to need a big drone to lug your high-end camera around and you are going to need a big wallet to pay for the repairs if you crash your DSLR-toting drone.

If you decide to go the route of a DSLR, there are several major manufacturers of DSLR cameras to consider like Pentax, Sony, Olympia, Nikon, and Canon. However, photo and video aficionados gravitate toward either Nikon or Canon, and you will hardly get an objective opinion from either on the merits of their camera of choice. So when it comes to picking your DSLR, focus on:

- **Sensor size:** The bigger the lens, the better the image. Full-frame sensors will capture images and video with greater detail and in a broader scale of light.

- **Available lens options:** One of the benefits of a DSLR is being able to swap out lenses. Canon and Nikon have a myriad of lens options to choose from and the quality of their lenses are in lock-step with the quality of their cameras

- **Image size (megapixels):** Lots of megapixels means lots of image information. Go big or go home!

- **Total weight:** One key indicator of the quality of your DSLR is the number of metal parts vs. plastic parts. The material wont impact the quality of the images rather it will impact the durability of the camera. When you're shopping for weight, plastic parts win out. Keep the weight down by using plastic lenses and use DSLRs that have more plastic parts.

Figure 3-9 provides a comparison of several popular DSLR makes and models.

Figure 3-9: Comparison of popular DSLR cameras.

Name	Nikon D5200	Nikon D3300	Pentax K-50	Sony Alpha 65 (SLT-A65VK)	Nikon D7100	Pentax K-3	Sony Alpha 77 (SLT-A77VQ)	Canon EOS 7D	Canon EOS 70D	Canon EOS 6D
Imensions	3.9 x 5.1 x 3.1 inches	3.9 x 4.9 x 3 inches	3.8 x 5.1 x 2.8 inches	3.9 x 5.25 x 3.25 inches	4.2 x 5.3 x 3 inches	3.9 x 5.2 x 3.1 inches	5.6 x 4.1 x 3.2 inches	4.4 x 5.8 x 2.9 inches	4.1 x 5.5 x 3.1 inches	4.4 x 5.7 x 2.8 inches
Weight	1.1 lb	15.2 oz	1.4 lb	1.4 lb	1.5 lb	1.8 lb	1.66 lb	1.8 lb	1.7 lb	1.66 lb
Type	D-SLR	D-SLR	D-SLR	D-SLR	D-SLR	D-SLR	D-SLR	D-SLR	D-SLR	D-SLR
Megapixels	24 MP	24 MP	16 MP	24 MP	24 MP	24 MP	24 MP	18 MP	20 MP	20 MP
Sensor Size	APS-C (23.5 x 15.6mm) mm	APS-C (23.2 x 15.4mm) mm	APS-C (23.5 x 15.6mm) mm	APS-C (23.5 x 15.6mm) mm	APS-C (23.5 x 15.6mm) mm	APS-C (23.5 x 15.6mm) mm	APS-C (23.5 x 15.6mm) mm	APS-C (23.5 x 15.6mm) mm	APS-C (22.5 x 15mm)	Full-Frame (36 x 24mm)
Maximum ISO	25600	25600	51200	16000	25600	51200	16000	12800	12800	102400
LCD size	3 inches	3 inches	3 inches	3 inches	3.2 inches	3.2 inches	3 inches	3 inches	3 inches	3 inches
LCD dots	921,000	921,000	921,000	921,600	1,228,800	1,037,000	920,000	920,000	1,040,000	1,040,000
Viewfinder Type	Optical	Optical	Optical	EVF	Optical	Optical	EVF	Optical	Optical	Optical
Video Resolution	720p, 1080i, 1080p	720p, 1080p	720p, 1080p	1080i, 1080p	720p, 1080p	720p, 1080i, 1080p	1080i, 1080p	720p, 1080p	720p, 1080p	720p, 1080p

Acquiring an action camera

Action cameras are small, durable cameras that were originally designed to give extreme sport enthusiasts a high-quality video camera to capture their hobbies up close and personally. Action cameras today are mounted to cars, mountain bikes, surf boards, and more. They are used to capture sky-diving, skateboarding, mountain biking, rock climbing, base jumping, fly fishing, and even more. They are versatile, powerful video cameras that have made movie making in crazy places a possibility.

These little cameras defy conventional wisdom that says that bigger is better. While the bigger sensors and bigger lenses are great for capturing deep, full, beautiful images, action cameras are capable of really wowing you with their video capabilities. In fact, the video footage is so good, that action cameras have actually been used to make major motion pictures like *The Need For Speed*. The driving scenes in this movie were almost exclusively filmed with GoPro cameras. Action cameras were designed precisely for being put in harms way, and that makes them a great match for drone use. Figure 3-10 shows several action cameras.

There are a lot of action cameras available today. Action cameras are extremely compact and therefore lack the physical space to incorporate a larger image sensor. These cameras also lack the option to change out or add on additional lenses. This means that your approach for selecting an action camera will be based off a different set of criteria than what you would use when picking a DSLR camera or point-and-shoot.

Figure 3-10: Action cameras are small but powerful.

Source: Andreas Kambanis/Creative Commons
Source: TechStage/Creative Commons

Action cameras need to be small so that they can ride along without greatly impacting the user. So they tend to lack a lot of the functionality that you might see with a DSLR or even a point-and-shoot. Since action cameras were designed with action in mind, they should have features that would be useful in capturing action footage like high-definition video modes. They should have high frame rates so that you can make beautiful slow-motion video clips, too. Streaming video feeds to a computer or monitor over Wi-Fi or Bluetooth is great for setting up your shot in the case that your camera is too compact to support an LCD.

Here is a list of features that you should take into consideration when picking your action camera:

- **Physical dimensions:** The smaller the better.

- **Total weight:** The smaller the better.

- **Maximum video resolution:** This number only matters at frame rates of 30 frames per second or higher.

    The higher the definition, the crisper and more vibrant the image will appear on your display device. At minimum this should be full HD (1080p).

- **Maximum frames per second:** The higher the number, the slower the slow-motion.

- **Waterproof depth rating:** If you take it swimming, this is how deep you can go before water will start seeping in.

- **Battery life:** It goes without saying that the longer the battery life, the more time you will spend flying instead of charging. Although a short battery life can be overcome if the battery is removable.

Figure 3-11 compares several action cameras available today. You'll notice that most of the prices are in the $200-$400 range. The GoPro Hero 4 Black, however, is nearly $500 but it comes loaded with features that have led to it being widely accepted and used by drone flyers around the globe.

	GoPro Hero4 Black	Drift Ghost-S	Sony AS100V	JVC Adixxion GC-XA2	Drift HD Ghost	Contour+ 2	Garmin Virb Elite	Ion Air Pro 3	Monoprice MHD Sport	IronX 5G9V HD
	$ 499.95	$ 364.21	$ 199.00	$ 299.00	$ 149.99	$ 265.67	$ 319.93	$ 197.99	$ 155.00	$ 164.00
Max Video Resolution	4k	1080p	1080p	1080p	1080p	1080p	1080p	1080p	1080p	1080p
Max Resolution at 30 fps	4k	1080p	1080p	1080p	1080p	1080p	1080p	1080p	1080p	1080p
Max Picture Resolution	12	12	13.5	16	11	5	16	12	5	5
Max Frames per Second	240	240	240	120	120	120	120	120	60	60
Max fps at 1080p	120	60	60	60	30	30	30	60	30	30
Max fps at 720p	120	120	120	120	60	60	60	120	60	60
Max HD Field of View	170	160	170	160	170	170	146	160	162	162
Battery Life	90	210	100	110	180	120	180	150	120	120
Weight	5.4	6	4.5	4.8	5.9	5.5	6.3	5	6.5	6.5
Interchangeable Battery?	X	X	X	X	X	X	X		X	X
App Controllable?	X	X	X	X	X	X	X	X	X	X
Wireless Connectivity?	X	X	X	X	X	X	X	X	X	X

Figure 3-11: Comparison of popular action cameras.

Balancing Features and Price

Choosing the camera with the right balance of features and price takes time and patience. If cost is the primary driver for you, then you may want to consider a point-and-shoot camera. These cameras are compact, low-cost, and heavy on the automatic features. The quality will not be what you can get with action cameras or DSLRs, but you will be able to get up and running for very little cost with this camera.

If you are primarily concerned with quality and money is not an issue then a DSLR may be for you. These cameras come with some automatic settings but the manual controls, large image sensors, and interchangeable lens options are why photo and video nerds flock to these devices. These cameras will give you seemingly endless options but at a high price.

Lastly, if budget is a concern and quality is a concern, there are numerous action cameras that may fit the bill. These cameras are small, powerful, and durable. They aren't as cheap as point-and-shoot cameras but they aren't anywhere near as expensive as DSLRs. They provide killer quality for the price point and are widely used and supported in the drone community.

Just remember, the drone you buy will inform the type of camera you can buy and the camera you buy will inform the type of drone you will have to buy.

Chapter 4

Finding Support and Resources

In This Chapter

▶ Finding and using drone communities online

▶ Joining a drone social group or Meetup

▶ Staying informed about drones with Google Alerts

Flight enthusiasts have been flying unmanned aerial vehicles since the 1940s. With the technological advancements, particularly with the advent of the modern day hobby drone, have come increasingly more interest in unmanned flight. With interest in drones growing seemingly exponentially, many people and resources are available to you that will make your flying experience much better than you might have experience in years past. Better batteries and advanced flight pilot and autopilot modes make flying a joy for novice hobby flyers!

This chapter shows you how to find drone communities online. You see how you can navigate them to find answers to technical questions, and get tips on how, when, and where to fly. Online communities are plentiful, and they serve as a useful tool for drone flyers around the globe.

Hobby flying is also a great way to meet people who have similar interests as you. In this chapter, you see how to navigate online discussion forums so that you can get answers quickly, and meet new people with ease. You also see how to find other flight enthusiasts in your area with social media and online services designed to get like-minded people together in the real world, not just the digital world.

The world of drones is constantly evolving and changing. The FAA has until September 2015 to come up with a set of rules and regulations to govern private and commercial drone use in the United States, which will also affect drone flyers in the EU and Canada. This chapter shows you how to get plugged in online so that you can stay informed on major topics like the evolving legal landscape and other pertinent topics of the time.

Finding and Navigating Online Communities

The only way to master flying a drone is to put in hours flying, crashing, and tinkering with it alongside educating yourself about the ins and outs of drones and drone flight. Your drone's manual and this book can help get you started, but in time, you will find that you need access to many more resources to help you excel at flying your drone. The good news is that many people like you all over the globe are pushing the limits with drones and drone technology, and they are connecting in online communities to share experiences.

A good place to find support for your drone is at its manufacturer's website. As more and more people fly a particular drone model, more bugs and quirks are found and funneled back to the manufacturer who can then quickly update its website. Needless to say, the manufacturer's website should be the most accurate, authoritative, and comprehensive source of information on your drone. Figure 4-1 is a screenshot of the support directory at DJI (the manufacturer of the Phantom line of drones). The support information on the DJI website is extensive, and of course, in case you can't find answers, they also provide support phone numbers and other contact methods. You may also find helpful information about your specific drone or drone's at large on other online communities that aren't manufacturer controlled or sponsored. These can be a great way to find tips and tricks that a manufacturer hasn't spent the time to uncover and suggest.

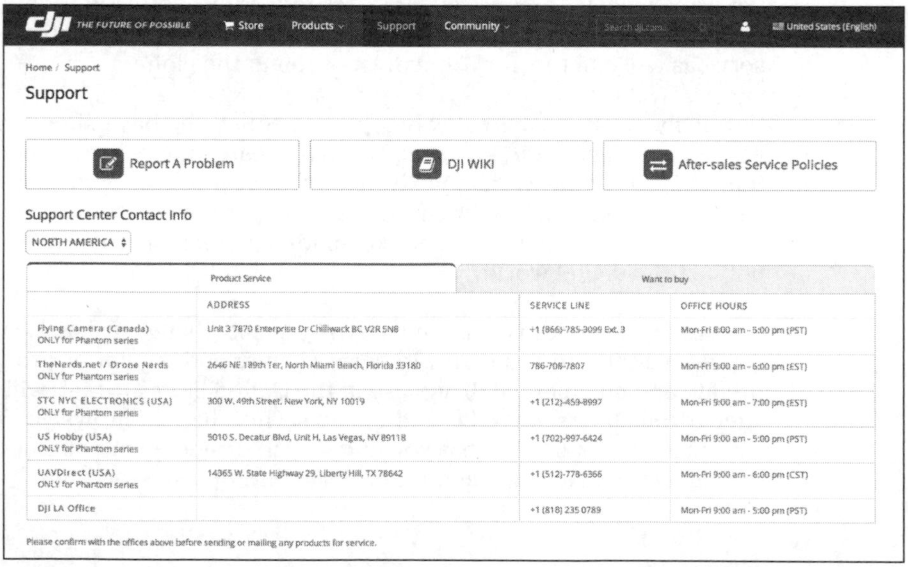

Figure 4-1: The DJI support directory.

Courtesy of Tucker Krajewski

Drone discussion forums

Sometimes support documentation or online FAQs (frequently asked questions) found on a manufacturer's website are overly technical or may not speak directly to your need. For that reason, you may find that traversing their user forums is the way to go. Forums are online communities of sorts where users can create a personal profile and post discussion topics where others in the forum community can weigh in with their thoughts and opinions. This is a great way to plug in with other enthusiasts online. If you are on a manufacturer forum, you will have a higher probability of finding someone that can help you use your drone better, faster.

WARNING!

Drone forums are great for getting input and feedback from real people, but unless the feedback you are getting is from a confirmed authority, meaning someone representing the manufacturer of your drone in an official capacity, take any and all input you receive with caution as it may be unqualified information that could potentially steer you, and your drone, into a tree.

Figure 4-2 is a screenshot of the forums on Parrot's website. As you can see in the figure, the forum is organized in a specific manner. At the highest level, everything in this discussion forum is about or relating to Parrot drones. Zooming in a little, there are then categories of forums. Each of the two Parrot drones has a category, and then a general community category is

Technical Support AR.Drone 2.0			
Forums	Topics	Posts	Last post
AR.Drone 2.0 Updates All about updates for your AR.Drone 2.0.	315	3,275	Today 13:50:20 by RaymuLam78
AR.Drone 2.0 Freeflight application All about AR.Drone Freeflight application (installation, content, uses, etc.)	414	2,841	Today 10:17:09 by DakortheaM
Hardware AR.Drone 2.0 All about AR.Drone spare parts and components.	953	7,292	Today 21:15:26 by usms
Software AR.Drone 2.0 All about AR.Drone applications (other than AR.Freeflight) and games.	255	1,519	Today 01:33:35 by jdg179

Technical Support AR.Drone			
Forums	Topics	Posts	Last post
AR.Drone Updates Update your AR.Drone	131	698	Today 09:53:22 by DakortheaM
AR.Drone Freeflight application All about AR.Drone Freeflight application (installation, ...)	109	519	Today 21:24:17 by usms
Hardware AR.Drone All about AR.Drone spare parts.	445	2,327	Today 03:53:07 by AbbeyCat
Software AR.Drone All about AR.Drone applications.	144	822	01-05-2015 18:15:52 by SlippySlope
FAQ Frequently asked questions about AR.Drone	120	510	12-13-2014 23:46:00 by mdh222

AR.Drone Community			
Forums	Topics	Posts	Last post
AR.Drone Photos Post here your best AR.Drone pictures.	154	738	Yesterday 04:44:31 by solaris8x86
Meet other pilots AR.Drone Fight against other AR.Drone pilots !	81	382	12-26-2014 05:19:20 by appleslizer6
AR.Drone Games All about AR.Drone Games.	14	65	09-30-2014 05:38:50 by Stella1
General All about PARROT AR.Drone.	664	3,040	Today 18:24:19 by slkrause

Figure 4-2: The Parrot drone forums.

Courtesy of Tucker Krajewski

included. Zoom in a little more and you will see that there are specific topics within categories. This helps with organizing the information being shared on specific topics in a category.

Each topic is a forum for discussion. When you find the topic that pertains to the topic you want to discuss, you can dive in and start searching for discussions that relate to your current interest or issue.

If your manufacturer does not have a discussion forum or maybe they do and the forum doesn't have much activity (if any at all), then you may want to cast a bigger net in the digital ocean. There are numerous drone discussion forums on the web that will help you connect with a milieu of people. Here are a few popular drone forums:

- ✔ `diydrones.com`
- ✔ `www.rcgroups.com`
- ✔ `www.dugn.org`

Understanding forum rules and etiquette

Forums are filled with interesting people who enjoy interacting with others while retaining some amount of anonymity. Online forum users tend to be fussy; they will let you know if you don't follow the rules. Yes, forums have rules. Before you start posting questions and discussion starters on an online forum, you should make sure you fully understand the rules of engagement. Figure 4-3 is a screenshot of some of the rules for the DJI forums. Some rules are obvious, like refraining from derogatory or defamatory speech, blatant advertising or spam, and so on. There are other rules that may not be as apparent, such as negative talk about the manufacturer, encouraging or demonstrating how to break the law with the manufacturers products, and so on.

Forums are typically policed by forum moderators who represent the forum owner and are tasked with monitoring the adherence to rules, settling grievances between users, and providing "expert" opinions and feedback. Understanding the forum rules should keep you out of the hot seat with the moderators. Forums are also typically self-policed by forum users. Following are some thoughts to keep in mind before you post in an online forum:

- ✔ **Read and understand the forum rules.** This will help keep you out of trouble with the forum moderators. Even if they don't catch an infraction, a fussy forum user will and they will likely report your devious behavior!

✔ **Be slow to speak.** Technology is making things happen so quickly these days that we are slowly losing the ability to exert a little patience. When you use a forum, search for your topic of interest before you post. If you post a duplicate discussion topic, you will likely frustrate other users.

✔ **Beware of trolls.** Forums are a great way to discuss issues with informed people. Forums are also a breeding ground for people that like to play games and suck others into useless debate and arguments, or even publicly humiliate them. These people are referred to as *trolls*. When you start posting in forums, tread lightly, and beware of lurking troublemakers.

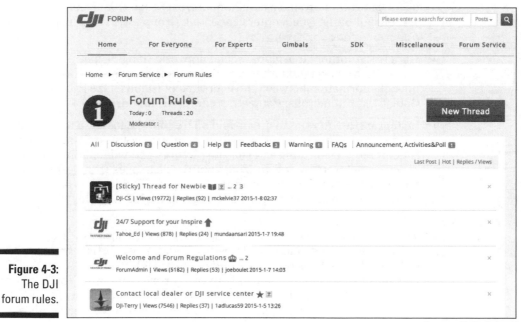

Figure 4-3:
The DJI
forum rules.

Courtesy of Tucker Krajewski

Using Social Media to Meet Drone Enthusiasts

Heard of Facebook? Then you likely have a general idea of what social media is. Wikipedia says that "social media is the social interaction among people in which they create, share, or exchange information, ideas, and more in virtual communities and networks." Sounds like a great place to meet other drone enthusiasts and experts, doesn't it? Social media isn't just for people; it is also for brands. Sometimes companies will interact with their customers and supporters more so on social media because of the residual impact it can have on brand awareness through the increased public chatter.

Whether you want to connect with people or companies, there are endless numbers of social networks all over the globe to help you. If you don't already have a social network of choice, here are a few to consider:

- **Facebook:** The largest global social network, Facebook is home to over 1.3 billion users. Create a personal profile, and connect with family, friends, colleagues, classmates, companies, public figures, and brands. Create discussion, share media, and otherwise be "social." Facebook is home to a seemingly infinite amount of special interest groups where users can gather around a common interest or passion. Figure 4-4 is a screenshot of the Quadcopters Facebook Group (www.facebook.com/groups/quadcopters).

- **Google+:** Another large global social network, Google+ has several features allowing users to better categorize their friends and control the flow of information between those groups of friends. Like Facebook, Google+ has numerous groups that center around drones.

- **Instagram:** If you want to create and share photos, Instagram is the platform for you. This social network is primarily a mobile-only network and is centered on capturing and sharing pictures and video. Connect with other drone users by categorizing your drone images with descriptive hashtags like #drones, #quadcopter, and so on. Figure 4-5 is a picture of someone navigating images on Instagram tagged with the #drones hashtag.

- **YouTube:** YouTube.com is the world's largest repository for video. Go to YouTube to find videos of almost anything. YouTube is a great place to find helpful videos on drones and connect with the drone enthusiasts making the videos. Publish your own drone content to YouTube to attract the attention of other flyers! YouTube also allows users to curate public content into channels that users can subscribe to. Figure 4-6 is a screenshot of a Channel search for drone content.

- **LinkedIn:** The leader in professional online networking, LinkedIn is connecting people professionally better than any other social network. One quick search for "Drones" will reveal professionals working in the UAV industry, LinkedIn groups for drone enthusiasts, drone companies, and more. Figure 4-7 shows several drone groups on LinkedIn.

When you search for drone groups on social media, try narrowing your focus to include more geographically specific group searches. For example, a quick search on Facebook for **Washington DC Drones** serves up the D.C. area Drone group. Finding a local group is a great way to get connected with drone users in your area.

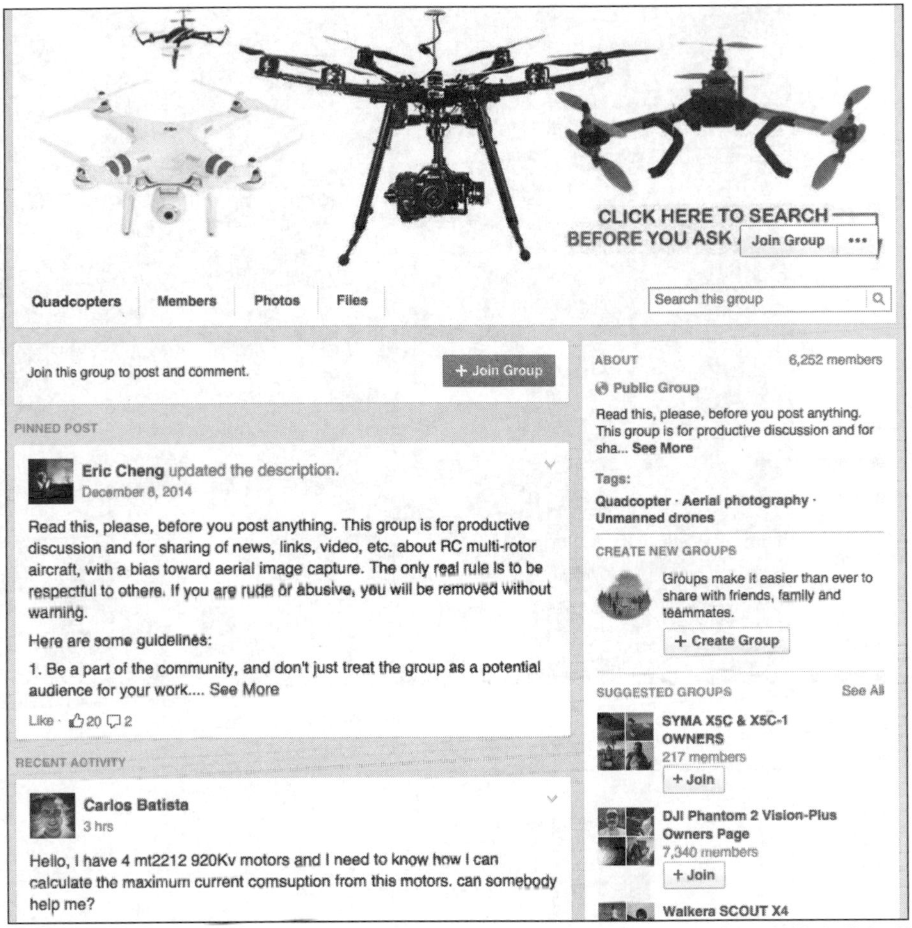

Figure 4-4:
Quad-
copters
Facebook
Group.

Courtesy of Tucker Krajewski

Drone Meetups

Meetup.com is a new social network that is designed to help people get together in real life. That's right, flesh and blood interaction is being aided by digital technology! Meetups.com is a great place to get plugged in with other drone flyers so that you can get out there and start flying.

Figure 4-8 shows the homepage for the Indianapolis drone flyers group. Residents of Indianapolis and nearby can join the group to interact with others online and get notified of events for the group.

Figure 4-5:
Instagram
is a network
of user-
curated
content.

Courtesy of Tucker Krajewski

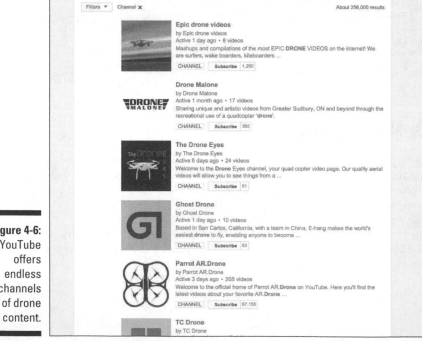

Figure 4-6:
YouTube
offers
endless
channels
of drone
content.

Courtesy of Tucker Krajewski

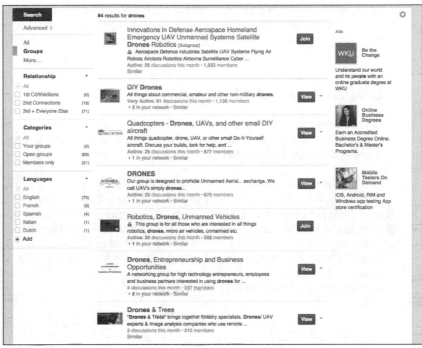

Figure 4-7: Searching for drone groups on LinkedIn yields pages of results.

Courtesy of Tucker Krajewski

Figure 4-8: Indianapolis drone flyers Meetup.

Courtesy of Tucker Krajewski

The great thing about Meetup.com is that they require you to commit to meeting in person. This is great for motivating people to get out there and socialize!

Google Groups

What doesn't Google do? Years ago, when smartphones exploded in popularity, people joked about how there was always "an app for that." Today, I just say there is a Google tool for that. Because there probably is.

Google Groups was designed to give people the opportunity to create their own discussion forum on specific topics. Google Groups allow you to get your own forum up and running with little technical knowhow. One great Google Groups feature is that users don't have to log in through a computer to access their group. Users can stay connected and correspond by email, meaning they never have to log into the Google Groups website. This is a great way to stay plugged in without ever having to log on! Figure 4-9 shows the Google Groups website.

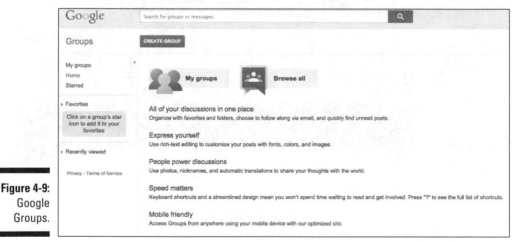

Figure 4-9:
Google
Groups.

Courtesy of Tucker Krajewski

Getting Drone News with Google Alerts

Using forums and social networks to connect with other drone users is a great way to not only get help with your drone and meet people, it's also a great way to stay informed on drone news. One major issue on the minds of most drone users is how the FAA's ruling in September 2015 will affect drone flying in the United States and around the world. If you are too busy to browse multiple forums, social media groups, and news outlets for drone news, you have options. Google has a tool called *Google Alerts* that is used to monitor the Internet for news stories that can then be emailed to you in real-time, daily, or weekly digests.

Enabling Google Alerts

To stay on top of drone news using Google Alerts, follow these steps:

1. **Using a computer or mobile web-enabled device, open your web browser and navigate to the following web address:**

   `https://www.Google.com/alerts`

   The Google Alerts web page opens. Here you can create alerts that will monitor the web for you. Figure 4-10 shows the Google Alerts website. Located toward the top of the web page is the search box where you will create an alert.

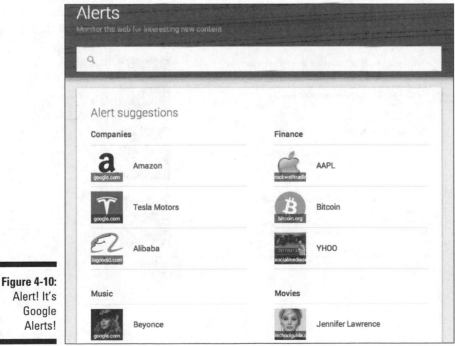

Figure 4-10: Alert! It's Google Alerts!

Courtesy of Tucker Krajewski

2. In the Alert box, enter a search term that would be relevant to the alert.

If you are interested in the FAA's progress toward establishing new laws, for example, try entering *FAA, Drones*. As you type your search terms, Google provides you with a preview of some of the content that would populate your alert today. The content loads underneath the Alert box. The preview results will contain an image, title, and a snippet of text, as shown in Figure 4-11.

Try the search term "FAA Drone Policy" or "FAA Drone Regulations 2015" for current policies governing drone usage. If you want to find out about new drone models being released, try using keywords related to manufacturer drones for example: "New DJI Drone" or "New Drone Model." If you want to get more specific, include the model year in your search term.

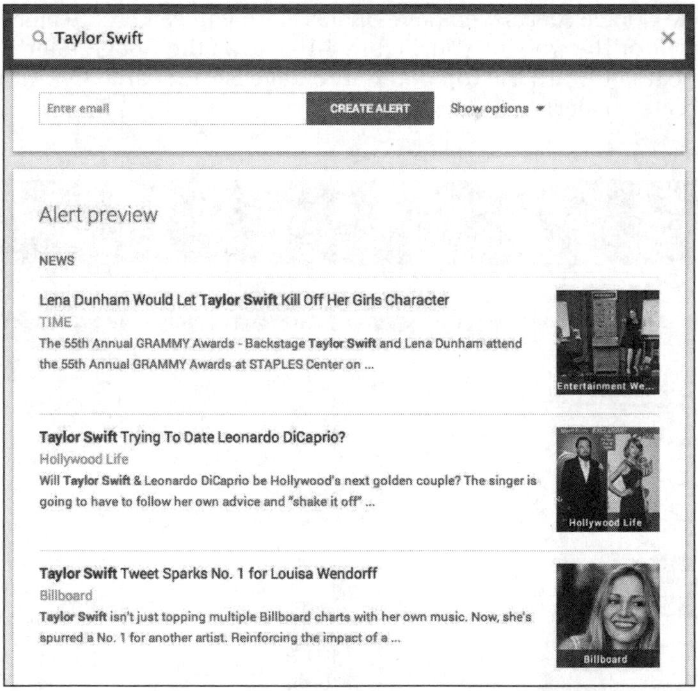

Figure 4-11:
Google
Alert results
preview.

Courtesy of Tucker Krajewski

3. **Customize the types of results and the frequency in-which you receive results by clicking the Options link located next to the Create Alert button.**

   An area that contains several options expands under your alert query. In this area, you will be able to customize your alert in the following ways:

   - **How often:** How frequently do you want Google to send alert results?

   - **Sources:** Specify whether you want general web content, news articles, blog posts, or other.

   - **Language:** Do you want only results in a specific language?

   - **Region:** Is there a part of the world that you are primarily interested in?

   - **How many:** You could get *every* result or just the most relevant. Choosing the most relevant results option will help keep you from being overwhelmed with Google alerts as they arrive in your Inbox.

4. **Create your alert by entering your email address in the form field located next to the Create Alert button, and then click Create Alert.**

   If a Google Account is associated with the email you entered, Google requires you to log in, and you may have to repeat the alert creation process. If your email address is not associated with a Google account, you receive a verification email so that you can verify your email is valid and active.

   The email address you assign for your Google Alerts should be an email address that you check at least at the frequency that you have opted to receive your alerts. Otherwise the alerts will pile up on you!

Deleting Google Alerts

If you would like to quickly delete your alert, you can do so by following these steps:

1. **Open an alert email that you have received from Google.**

2. **Scroll to the bottom of the email to locate the unsubscribe link.**

   Click the link to unsubscribe from the alert. You will be taken to a web page asking you to confirm your decision to unsubscribe from the alert, as shown in Figure 4-12.

3. **If you are positive you would like to unsubscribe, click Unsubscribe.**

   You are unsubscribed from the alert and will no longer receive notifications.

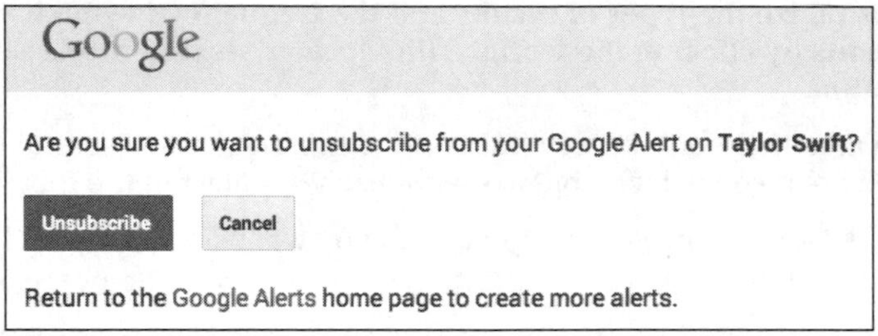

Courtesy of Tucker Krajewski

Figure 4-12: Are you sure you want to unsub- scribe?

Editing Google Alerts

If you created your alert with a Google account, you have some additional options beyond simply deleting alerts. You can reconfigure the alert's options by editing the search query. To edit an alert created with your Google Account, follow these steps:

1. **Using a computer or mobile web-enabled device, open your web browser and navigate to the following web address:**

   `https://www.Google.com/alerts`

   The Google Alerts web page opens, where you can create alerts that will monitor the web for you. If you are not logged in, the Create Alert button that appears on this page will be accompanied by an email address text field. If you see this text field, you will need to log in to your Google Account.

2. **If you are not logged in, click the *Sign In* button located in the top right corner of the browser window.**

   The Google login page opens, where you are presented with a field for entering your email address and password.

3. **Enter the correct email address and password, then click Enter.**

   Your browser automatically redirects to the Google Alerts page where you will be presented with the option to create a new alert or edit your existing alerts.

4. **Edit your alert by clicking the corresponding pencil icon located on the right side of the alert list.**

   An area containing several options will expand giving you the option to modify the alert query, and the options associated with the alert as shown in Figure 4-13.

5. **When you are satisfied with your changes, click Update Alert to save your changes.**

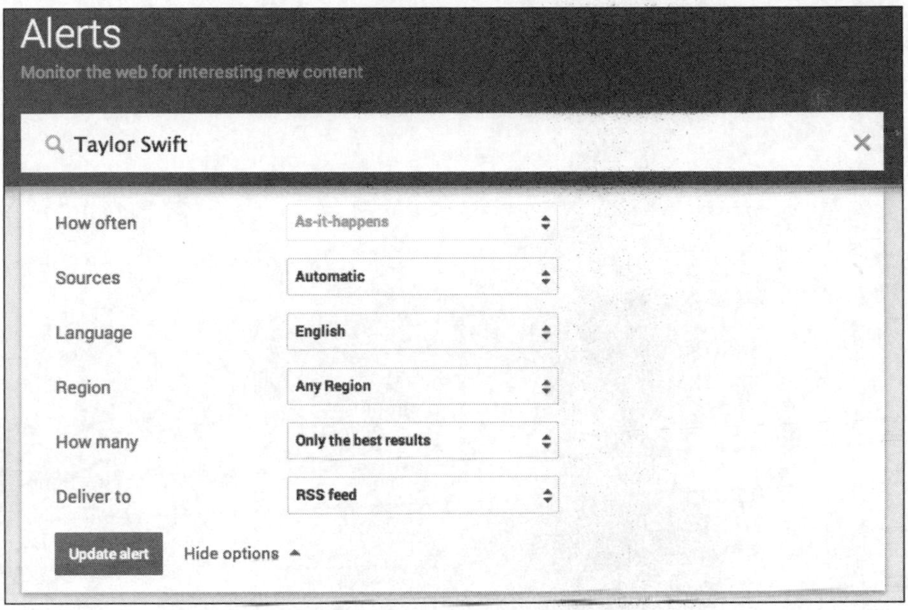

Courtesy of Tucker Krajewski

Figure 4-13: Editing your alert.

Part II
Before You Fly

In This Part . . .

✔ Setting up your drone

✔ Following basic safety guidelines

✔ Being aware of the law

Chapter 5

Setting Up Your Drone

In This Chapter

▶ Unboxing and inspecting your drone

▶ Exploring your drone's components

▶ Configuring your camera

*W*hen you buy a drone, you must research the features and price of many drones to find one that suits your needs. For the most part, drones that you get from DJI, 3D Robotics, or Parrot will be ready-to-fly, meaning they come complete with everything you need to fly. Typically, some assembly is involved, but this isn't much more than attaching a camera, batteries, and propellers.

Other drones, called bind-and-fly drones, do not come with a transmitter and typically require more setup. Bind-and-fly drones are sold by drone companies that target the more engineering savvy drone flyer. They are very customizable and designed for more advanced users.

This chapter explores setting up and configuring the less complex ready-to-fly drones. The chapter walks you through unboxing your drone and taking an inventory of all its parts and instructions. Then you assemble your drone and update its software. In this chapter, you also see how to configure your drone's integrated camera to take the best possible aerial photos and video.

If your drone supports an add-on camera, don't fret. You also see how to attach your camera to your drone. In the case of more advanced drones, you learn about gimbals and how to attach one to your drone, and attach your camera to your gimbal.

Unboxing Your Drone

Your drone comes with several parts that you want to be sure not to lose. Depending on the type of drone you purchased, your parts list could include all, some, or more of the items in the following sections.

Propellers

Propellers are blades that, when attached to a drone, spin to create lift and take the drone to the skies. Propellers are rarely packaged already attached to a drone. They could become damaged in shipping, and they would greatly increase the drone's packaging needs. Propellers are durable yet fragile, so don't leave them in a place where they can be damaged. Set them on something like an end table, countertop, or coffee table so that no one sits or steps on them.

Propellers are typically made from plastic, although high-end propellers are sometimes made from carbon fiber. Rigid and lightweight propellers tend to perform better than heavier propellers that flex. Also, some drones come with special propellers that self-tighten when in use. These are particularly useful for the novice user who may not know the appropriate amount of torque to apply to the propellers when fastening them to the drone. Figure 5-1 shows the DJI Phantom 2 Vision's propellers. These propellers are self-tightening plastic propellers. They can be replaced with slightly larger custom carbon fiber propellers, but doing so requires technical knowhow and confidence.

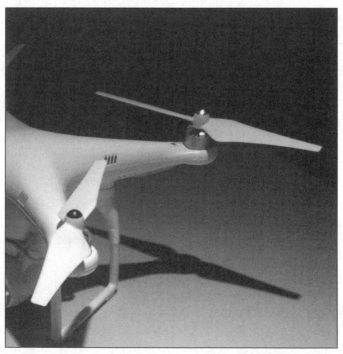

Figure 5-1:
DJI self-tightening propellers are great for first time flyers.

Source: Stephan Ridgway/Creative Commons

Motor

Propellers are attached directly to the drone's motors. There is no complex drive chain involved with most drones, which is great for conserving energy and removing potential break points. A drone's motors spin at an extremely high rate of speed so that the propellers can create lift. The motors are controlled by a computer that is housed inside the airframe of your drone. The computer controls the motors, and each motor works independently to ensure the stability of the drone. By varying the speed of each motor, the drone is able to hover in place, climb or descend, and move in all directions.

Your drone will come packaged with a motor that is optimized specifically for your particular drone; however, motors do fail, and therefore, you may need to replace it at some point. Drone motors come in standard sizes but with different levels of power output and energy conservation. Your drone may support different motors that give you more speed than the stock motors that came with your drone. Figure 5-2 shows the motors in a Pocket Drone. Notice that the motors are neatly enclosed in the end of the arm of the drone. This is to help shield the motor from the elements and bad piloting.

Figure 5-2:
Motors in
a Pocket
Drone.

Source: Airdroid

Aircraft Airframe

Every part of the drone is somehow connected to the airframe. Some drone airframes are designed to encapsulate every aspect of the drone, whereas some hold only the "brains." Figure 5-3 shows the DJI Phantom 2 drone. This airframe provides a protective shell over the drone computer, battery, and wiring. The landing gear is affixed to the airframe, and the drone itself has mounts for a camera gimbal (more on that later). Breaking your airframe is a big deal. It's on par with bending your car frame in an accident.

Figure 5-3: The DJI Phantom 2 airframe is designed to protect its electrical components like the computer and navigational sensors.

Source: B Ystebo/Creative Commons

Battery and charger

Every drone should come packaged with a battery and a battery charger. Drone batteries are high-power Lithium Polymer (LiPo for short) batteries. They are designed to store and release a load of energy! To do this, the batteries use a relatively volatile cocktail of chemicals. These batteries are fragile so you need to take great care when using them. Your drone should come with a battery charger designed specifically for your drone's batteries. Overcharging a drone battery can make it swell and burst into flames, causing wicked amounts of damage. Your drone's battery charger should be designed specifically for your drone's batteries and should have several safety features:

- ✔ Automatic shutoff at 100% charge
- ✔ Storage mode or discharge
- ✔ Compatibility check

If you plan to buy additional batteries, be sure to purchase batteries recommended by your drone manufacturer. If they do not provide a recommended list of batteries, you will need to check to make sure the batteries you use have the same features as the batteries that came packaged with your drone. Doing so will help safeguard you from harm. Some manufacturers remove this variable by making a proprietary battery that you can purchase only from them. The benefit is that you can't use the wrong battery. The downside is that you may have to pay a premium to buy additional batteries. Figure 5-4 shows the Parrot AR 2.0 Drone battery. This battery is designed specifically for the AR 2.0 drone.

Figure 5-4: Stay safe and buy batteries designed specifically for your drone.

Source: Tokyo Times/Danny Choo/Creative Commons

Protective hull and prop guards

Propellers are thin and light. They are constructed from rigid materials and spin at extremely high rates. All of this combined makes them extremely hazardous to your health. Getting your finger in the path of a spinning drone blade could cut easily cut your finger down to the bone or sheer it off completely (ouch!). A great way to avoid this happening is to simply never put your fingers near the propellers when they are moving. If you want to be even more cautious, stay away when the battery is plugged in! You can also give yourself, and your drone, a little additional protection by using a protective hull or prop guards.

These guards are designed to protect you from your propellers and also protect your drone's propellers from you and other objects. Drones are extremely stable but not as stable as a car that is driving down the road. Drones are easily blown around by air currents, which can cause them to bump into people and things. You might recall from the previous section, "Propellers," that propellers are rather fragile. Prop guards and protective hulls like the ones pictured in Figure 5-5, provide an additional layer of protection for the drone in the event the unexpected happens and it gets friendly with a tree or a wall or you. But remember, they are not foolproof and you can still damage yourself, people, and objects when using the prop guards.

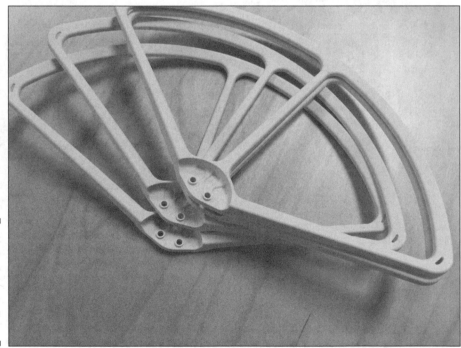

Figure 5-5:
Protective hulls keep you and your drone safe from injury.

Courtesy of Andrew Amato

Camera mount and gimbal

You may recall from Chapter 2 that many drones are built with an integrated camera. That means you don't have to worry about buying and attaching a camera to your drone. Other drones give you the option to add on a camera.

Attaching a camera to your drone may require the assistance of a special mount. Depending on your drone, this may be a simple bracket that secures a camera like a GoPro to the body of your drone. High-end mounts are called gimbals and if your drone supports a gimbal, you're in luck! Gimbals are designed to keep your camera perfectly level and stable while airborne. Chapter 13 goes into detail on how to use a gimbal to stabilize your footage. Figure 5-6 is a picture of the gimbal that comes with the DJI Phantom 2. It is designed precisely for carrying a GoPro action camera.

Figure 5-6:
DJI
Phantom's
GoPro
gimbal is top
notch!

Source: bjoern.gramm/Creative Commons

Transmitter

For the purposes of this chapter and this book, we are mainly discussing drones that are ready-to-fly. That means that they come with a transmitter that is connected to the drone and requires no additional setup. All drone flight controllers have the same basic core controls which consist of two sticks that give you complete directional control.

Innovations in wireless communication (GPS, Bluetooth, and Wi-Fi), have made it possible to control some drones with devices other than a traditional flight controller, such as a mobile phone, computer, or tablet. Chapter 8 provides more information on this topic.

Instruction manual

Your drone should come packaged with a user manual. Some drones are packaged with a few different manuals so as to keep excessively advanced topics separate from the bare necessities. I hope my wife doesn't read this part of the book because I am going to suggest something I never do: Read the manual before you attempt to assemble anything. Your drone likely has several quirks and your manual will explain them in detail.

Most manuals start with all the necessary warnings, just to get your attention and to make sure you proceed with caution. Use your manual to ensure that the contents of your package are complete and accurate. Your manual should also give you a brief tour of all of the different parts of your drone and their intended purpose. Most manuals give step-by-step setup instructions and finish with a brief explanation of the controls and how to get airborne. Figure 5-7 shows a couple of pages from the DJI Phantom manual. Before you ask a single question about how to fly your drone, make sure you read the manual.

Figure 5-7: The DJI Phantom quick start manual.

Courtesy of Tucker Krajewski

Assembling Your Drone

Every drone available on the market today comes with its own set of assembly instructions. Some drones require more installation steps than others. Typically, you need to install the following items:

✔ **Propellers:** Your drone should be packaged with at least one complete set of propellers and possibly even a spare propeller or two. When you install the propellers, be sure that you carefully read the instructions to ensure that you put the propeller with the correct side up. Be sure to use the correct nuts to secure the propeller and tighten each nut with the appropriate amount of pressure. You don't want your propellers to be loose. Conversely, overtightening can fracture your propellers.

DJI drones indicate on the propeller which side of the propeller to face upward, as well as the direction to spin the propeller to tighten it. 3D Robotics differentiates propellers with different colored nuts.

✔ **Landing gear:** Most drones are packaged with their landing gear unattached, so be sure to securely attach the landing gear to the drone. Landing gear is critical for the stability of the drone. In some drone models, it provides ground clearance for any camera gear that might be bottom mounted. Be sure to refer to your manual to ensure that your gear is affixed appropriately, especially if it is retractable landing gear.

✔ **Camera gear:** If you haven't flown a drone yet, you may want to get a few flights under your belt before strapping on a camera. Depending on your drone, you will either attach the drone's camera package or you will attach the mount or gimbal for your own camera. Be sure to follow the instructions precisely when mounting your camera. The placement of the camera is critical for maintaining stability.

Charging batteries

LiPo Batteries are far more volatile than most batteries and therefore require a little more TLC. To safely transport or store your drone batteries, you must be sure to they are at least 50% discharged. The more charged they are, the more flammable they are. Also, fully charged LiPo batteries that go unused for more than a day or so run the risk of wearing down their capacity and therefore dramatically reducing their useful life. For these reasons, your drone batteries will have half-charge or less when you take them out of the box. Charging your batteries can take a little time so you want to get the process started sooner than later. Refer to your manual to confirm the best practices for your battery and charger. Figure 5-8 shows a LiPo battery charger. This style of charger is commonly packaged with drones.

Be sure to monitor your batteries as they charge for the first time to ensure that all the safety features of your battery charger do indeed work. Your battery charger should indicate that charging is complete and the battery is fully charged. Your charger should also indicate if there is an issue with charging. Pay attention to these indicators to avoid potential calamity.

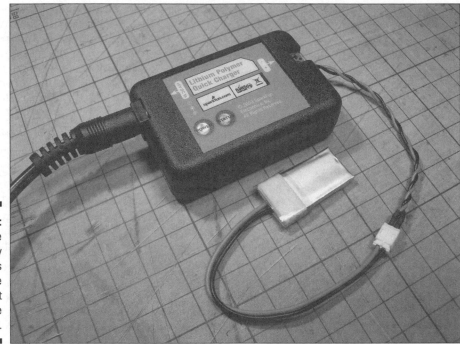

Figure 5-8:
Drone
battery
chargers
look the
same but
may be
different.

Source: Osamu Iwasaki/Creative Commons

If you do not have any instructions for how to charge your batteries, use the following tips to stay safe:

- ✔ Before you plug your charger into a power source, look it over to see if there is any voltage mode that needs to be set first. You may need to switch the voltage mode so that it matches with your country's power system. In the U.S., you would want it set to 110 volt.

- ✔ Locate the various status indicators so that you know where to look when you plug the charger into a power source and then plug the battery (or batteries) into the charger. Indicators will let you know if all is good or if something is getting sideways on you.

- ✔ If your LiPo battery has power leads running off of it, make sure they never touch each other as this could cause your battery to short circuit.

- ✔ Check the indicator to see if there is any sort of a battery type indicator. If so, make sure the option selected matches the battery you intend to charge. In most cases, this will be LiPo.

If you get the impression that something is going awry when you charge your battery, unplug the charger from the power source before doing anything else, and then see Chapter 6 for tips on how to stay safe with your LiPo batteries.

Checking for software updates

A great deal of high-end hardware goes into making a drone capable of flight. Modern drones contain internal computers with software flight controllers that use a milieu of sensors to gather information necessary to facilitate flight. Many newer drones are also using their GPS and internal mapping software to ensure that you aren't flying in restricted airspace. This hardware and software are all very high-tech, and both are getting even more advanced.

With computers, you need to update the software periodically to ensure that you get the most from your device. Drones are no different. Drone manufacturers are constantly making improvements to the software that powers their drones. Before you are ready to fly, you must ensure that your drone is using the most current software available. Updating your drone's software is important because the manufacturer may have found bugs or upgraded the flight controller's intelligence, and you will want to take advantage of those advancements.

If you have a DJI Phantom 2 Drone, you can upgrade the software in your drone and in your remote control by following these steps. You will need a USB cable to connect your drone to your computer, and you will need an Internet connection to download the assistant software and any available firmware updates.

 If you already installed propellers, you should consider removing them before starting the upgrade process. Upgrading your drone requires it and the controller to be powered on. Removing the propellers will protect you and others from accidents that could occur when your device is powered on.

1. **Using your computer, navigate to the following web address:**

   `http://www.dji.com/product/phantom-2/download`

   You should arrive at the DJI support download page. Manuals for their devices are located at the top of the page, and software is located at the bottom of the page. All downloads are listed with their release dates.

2. **Locate the most current release version of the assistant software and download it by clicking the `Zip` link for windows and `DMG` link for Mac.**

   The software downloads to the location on your computer that you specified.

3. **Install the assistant software by double-clicking on the install file that you just downloaded.**

   The file will unzip revealing an install file.

4. **If you are on a Mac, drag the Phantom logo to the application folder, as shown in Figure 5-9. If you are on a PC, double click the unzipped executable file denoted by the .*exe* extension file.**

   Follow the prompts to complete the Phantom 2 Software installation on your machine.

5. **Plug your drone battery into your drone.**

   Ensure that your battery has a full charge so that it can keep your drone powered for the duration of the installation process.

6. **Locate the USB port on your remote control and the USB port on your drone, place a USB cable into each device, and plug each device into your computer.**

   If your computer has only one USB port available, start with the remote control.

7. **With your drone and/or remote control plugged into your computer, launch the Phantom assistant software.**

   The Phantom software searches for any new firmware updates. If any are available, it prompts you to confirm installation.

8. **Follow the prompts to complete the upgrade process.**

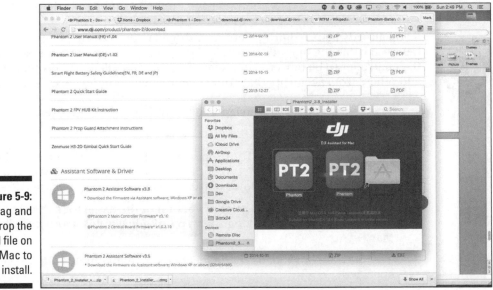

Figure 5-9:
Drag and drop the install file on your Mac to install.

Courtesy of Mark LaFay

Getting Familiar with Your Aerial Camera

The setup process for a drone with an integrated camera is seamless compared to that for drones without integrated cameras. Chances are good that an integrated camera pales in comparison to a camera like a GoPro or other high-end digital camera, but you can still capture fantastic photos and videos with it. Not to mention, what an integrated camera lacks in photo and video quality, it makes up for in usability and features.

Here are the two most popular drones currently on the market that come with integrated cameras and some of their features and options:

- **Parrot AR 2.0 Drone.** The video controls for the Parrot AR 2.0 Drone are somewhat limited. You do not have the option to adjust the video mode for the camera, but you do have high-end control features. Parrot refers to these controls as *Director Mode.* To take advantage of the photo and video capabilities of the AR 2.0, you will need to pilot the craft with your smartphone or tablet. The camera comes already connected and calibrated; all you need to do is install the app on your phone and pair your phone with the drone. To do this, refer to your drone's user manual.

- **DJI Phantom 2 Vision and Phantom 2 Vision+ drones.** DJI is the clear industry leader in drone technology, and while their integrated cameras are superior to the AR Drones, they still lack a little in picture quality and custom controls compared to an action camera like a GoPro. The Phantom 2 Vision does not come with a gimbal-mounted camera, so the video can be shakier than the footage gathered from a Phantom 2 Vision+, which does sport a nice camera and gimbal. The Phantom 2 application also gives the user the ability to change minor features like resolution and field of view. These features are nice but limited. Refer to your user manual to pair your mobile phone to the Phantom 2 Vision and to control your camera.

You don't have to get airborne to test your camera; in fact, you should snap a few photos to ensure the device is fully functioning before you put it in the sky.

Using a GoPro

You can use several types of cameras with drones; however, the GoPro has received the most widespread support simply because the camera's technology and capabilities are regarded as the best in the action camera market. For this reason, this book focuses largely on GoPro cameras as the camera of choice for aerial photography and video.

You can mount a GoPro to a drone in several ways. Your drone manufacturer may specify proprietary mounting systems, or they may rely on existing GoPro mounting technology. To be sure you have the right equipment, you should refer to your device manual.

Here are three ways you can mount a GoPro to a drone:

✔ **Direct mount:** Some drones have a bracket designed to attach the GoPro in its protective case to the drone. Figure 5-10 is a picture of the GoPro camera in a waterproof case with a mounting adapter.

The Pocket Drone is designed to be extremely small but powerful and does not support a fancy mounting rig or gimbal. To save on weight, the Pocket Drone is equipped with a shock-mounted plate where you can affix a GoPro Mounting bracket with adhesive as shown in Figure 5-11. You'll also notice that in these types of mountings, unless you have a GoPro case designed with a mount point on the top, your footage will be upside down. This can be fixed by changing the Upside Down Mode (UPd) setting in capture settings.

✔ **Camera frames:** Some drones offer their own proprietary mounting system. For example, the DJI Phantom supports a mounting frame. The GoPro is seated and secured in a special adapter as shown in Figure 5-12. The adapter is then mounted to the bottom of the Phantom. You'll notice that the mounting system for the Phantom does not allow you to mount the GoPro in its protective case. The camera is, however, right-side-up, which means that you won't have to deal with any inverted video footage or stills.

✔ **Gimbal:** Gimbals are high-end mounting systems that reduce shake by stabilizing the camera. Some gimbals also provide remote control of the camera so that you can adjust the angle for the camera and even rotate to capture different perspectives. Using your GoPro with a Gimbal will provide you with the highest quality footage. Your drone manufacturer will suggest which gimbals are optimized specifically for their equipment so refer to your drone manual before you buy. Figure 5-13 shows the 3D Robotics Iris+, complete with a GoPro supported Gimbal.

Gimbals tend to reduce flight time due to their weight. Be sure to reference your drone's user manual to determine how much flight time loss to compensate for.

Figure 5-10:
GoPro
camera
cases have
mounting
technology
that accom-
modate a
number of
different
uses cases,

Source: TAKA@P.P.R.S/Creative Commons

Figure 5-11:
Mount your
go pro to
a pocket
drone with
adhesive.

Courtesy of TJ Johnson

Figure 5-12:
The Phantom GoPro mounting frame is a nice low-cost solution for flying a GoPro.

Source: bjoern.gramm/Creative Commons

Figure 5-13:
Iris+ flies a gimbal and a GoPro.

Source: Christopher Michel/Creative Commons

Configuring your GoPro

Before you can capture cinema quality photos and video, you must configure your GoPro. You can configure your GoPro by navigating the small screen on the front of the device. Or you can use the GoPro mobile application, if you have an Apple, Android, or Windows smartphone. Once installed on your phone, the GoPro app gives you the ability to remotely configure camera settings, livestream video from the camera, and even share content to the web. You can also start and stop video recording and snap photos remotely with the mobile app.

If you want to control your GoPro with your smartphone, you must first download the app to your mobile device from your device's app store. The process for pairing your phone to the GoPro varies depending on the version of GoPro you have and the type of phone you have. To get detailed instructions for all devices, visit GoPro Support online here: `http://gopro.com/support/articles/getting-started-with-gopro-app`.

If you don't have a smartphone available, you can also use a GoPro remote, shown in Figure 5-14, to control your GoPro while it is flying high on your drone. The remote will give you control of the camera distances topping nearly 600 feet. Snap photos, start and stop video, and configure you camera on the fly with the remote.

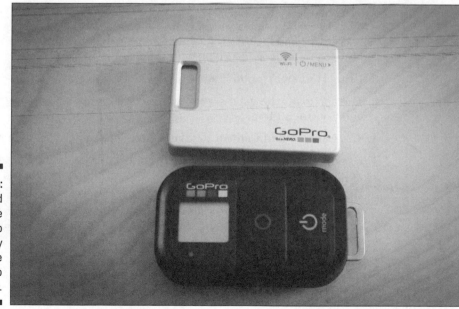

Figure 5-14: Control and configure your GoPro remotely with the GoPro Remote.

Before you purchase the GoPro remote, you should consult your drone's user manual to ensure that your GoPro's Wi-Fi will not interfere with your Drone's wireless communication system. The DJI Phantom drones do not play nicely with GoPro Wi-Fi and therefore you can't use the app or the remote.

If your drone does not support wireless control, then your next best bet is to set the GoPro to record just prior to taking off. When you land your drone, you will need to stop the recording. The downside to this is that you will have to process a video file that is as long as your flight from takeoff to landing. The GoPro Hero4 Black shoots in several video modes going all the way up to 4k which is essentially 4 times bigger than High Definition video which is commonly referred to as 1080p. The settings in 4k are somewhat restrictive and the files are so big they can be nearly impossible to work with for some computers, therefore, the best setting to get you started is 1080p Video at 60 frames per second (FPS), and a narrow field of view (FOV).

To configure your GoPro Hero4 with the settings detailed above using your mobile phone, follow these steps:

1. **Turn your GoPro on so that your smartphone can detect it.**

   The GoPro camera indicator screen should light up and indicate that it is powered on. Unless you configured your GoPro camera otherwise, it should also flash blue to indicate that Wi-Fi is on.

2. **Connect your smartphone to the GoPro camera's Wi-Fi.**

   You should see the Wi-Fi from the GoPro camera listed under your wireless connections from your smartphone. You may need to set up the Wi-Fi name and password on your GoPro camera; for instructions on how to do this, see the manual for your GoPro camera.

3. **Using your smartphone, launch the GoPro application.**

   The app loads the main screen with several options, including a Connect and Control button.

4. **Tap Connect and Control to take control of your GoPro camera.**

   If your phone is able to successfully connect to your GoPro camera, the app loads a streaming video feed from your GoPro camera and presents you with several options for controlling your GoPro camera remotely.

5. **To configure your Camera, tap the wrench icon located in the bottom of the screen. On an iPhone, this is located in the bottom right as shown in Figure 5-15.**

   The Configuration screen loads, giving you several options for your camera.

Figure 5-15:
The settings button is in the bottom right side of the camera control screen on the GoPro app for iPhone.

Courtesy of Mark LaFay

6. **In the Video Settings section of the configuration screen, locate and tap Resolution and change the resolution to 1080p (not 1080p Superview).**

   The setting changes, and then you are returned the configuration menu.

7. **In the Video settings section of the configuration screen, locate and tap FPS (Frames Per Second), and set it to 60. If you have an older model GoPro camera, you may top out at 30. This is acceptable, as well.**

   The setting will change and then you will be returned the configuration menu.

8. **In the Video settings section of the configuration screen, locate and tap FOV (Field of View) to change it to Narrow.**

   This will remove the fish-eye effect that can appear on GoPro footage when the FOV is set to Medium or Wide.

9. **Locate the Done button at the top of the screen and tap it to return to the camera control screen.**

Configuring your GoPro camera will be a little bit of a chore, mainly because the screen and buttons are so small. But once you've gotten your GoPro camera configured and connected to your smartphone, getting up and running each time you fly will be fast and easy.

Chapter 6

Staying Safe with Your Drone

. . . .

In This Chapter

▶ Knowing the imminent dangers with drones

▶ Exploring how to avoid propeller dangers

▶ Identifying the quirks of your drone to avoid accidents

▶ Avoiding fires with proper battery care

. . . .

*F*or most people, safety is something that can never be overlooked. In fact, it is a major driver in deciding what things to buy or not buy for themselves or for their loved ones. Maybe this is you. Maybe you are Ralphie's mom in *A Christmas Story,* always worried that someone might shoot an eye out.

It's funny to think about, but you can't really discount safety. It is important that you always understand the dangers inherent with every activity in which you are participating. Potential dangers shouldn't prevent you from participating in a given activity; it should just drive how you participate. Are fireworks dangerous? Absolutely. Can they be used safely? Absolutely!

The good news is that you can't blow your hands off with a drone. Nor can you shoot your eye out. However, you *can* burn your house down, harm other people, poke an eye out, cut off fingers (or worse), cause car accidents and plane crashes, and ruin birthday parties and weddings. But don't worry, that's only if you don't know what you are doing when you use your drone. The more experience you get with your drone, the safer you will become. But there is that whole inexperienced phase that you and the world around you need to be wary of. There are common sense things you can do to stay safe and then there are things that you will learn with time.

In this chapter, you learn about imminent dangers with your drone and how to safely navigate those dangers. Respect your drone propellers for the havoc they can wreak. Protect yourself and others from propeller accidents that can land you in the emergency room. Avoid accidents with your drone by learning how different features that are designed for your benefit can cause unintended accidents when not used properly. And last, explore how drone batteries work, what makes them great for use with drones, and how to properly use them so that they do not catch fire or explode.

The consumer drone market is a relatively new one, and it is growing at a rapid pace. There several mass-manufactured drones hitting the shelves thanks to companies like DJI, 3D Robotics, and Parrot. These drones come with many safety mechanisms in place designed to keep you and others free from harm. There is also a burgeoning community of hobbyists that are building drones from scratch, and in some cases for sale. Figure 6-1 is a picture of a custom built drone that is built for speed and power! These drones are designed to be more customizable by the end-user and they may not come with all of the failsafe features that the big manufacturers build into their devices.

Regardless of the drone you have or intend to purchase, there are several obvious dangers associated with using a drone. For this reason, drones shouldn't be regarded as innocuous toys; rather, they should be respected and used with great care. Doing so will help you avoid unnecessary damage to your drone and personal injury.

Figure 6-1:
Custom
drones
can be
designed for
numerous
uses.

Source: Intel Free Press/Creative Commons

Avoiding Propeller Injuries

Propellers are the blades that are attached to the motors of your drone. When power is applied to the motors, the propellers spin at a high rate of speed. The rotation of the propeller forces air down toward the ground.

This flow of air changes the relative air pressure above and below the propellers, which in turn creates lift, and your drone becomes airborne.

The size and weight of the drone largely dictate the number and size of propellers needed as well as the speed at which the propellers must spin to achieve flight. Small drones don't pose a great risk of injury because the propellers are small, soft, and don't rotate with nearly as much force as their big brothers, but they are still dangerous. Big drones, however, pose a great safety risk because the propellers are larger and typically made out of rigid material, such as hard plastics or carbon fiber. Coming in contact with a spinning propeller on a drone like a Parrot AR 2.0 or DJI Phantom 2 could result in substantial harm. You are almost guaranteed to be lacerated and depending on the impact this could require stitches or worse. Don't take my word for it; Google *drone propeller injuries* and take a look at the images that are served up.

It goes without saying, don't stick your hands, feet, or other objects in the path of a moving propeller. Propellers are necessary for flight, and you can't cover them up completely because you need to be able to move air through the propellers to create lift. There are a few safety precautions that are built into most drones, or can be easily added.

Propeller guards and protective hulls

Major drone manufacturers such as DJI and Parrot build several safety mechanisms into their devices. The popular DJI Phantom drones come with propeller guards that are designed to provide a level of protection from propeller injuries that result from side impacts. In the event that your drone takes off and you or others are standing too close, an unexpected breeze could blow the drone into you, causing serious injury. The propeller guard provides some protection from this sort of scenario. Figure 6-2 shows a propeller guard that is used with the DJI Phantom drones.

Parrot took safety a step further by creating a protective hull that attaches to the drone and pretty much turns it into an aerial bumper car. The hull is Styrofoam, so it adds negligible weight to the drone. It also provides quite a bit of protection. Figure 6-3 is a picture of the hull Parrot uses to cover the entire drone, including all four propellers.

You should notice and be aware that because the flow of air is top-down through the propellers, the props cannot be completely covered. Common sense tip number one is to not stick your fingers into moving propellers.

Figure 6-2:
Propeller
guards
will pro-
vide some
protection
from
spinning
propellers.

Source: B Ystebo/Creative Commons, Christopher Michel/Creative Commons

Safety indicators

Every drone has its own set of safety indicators, and you need to know what these are before you operate your drone. To learn how to identify where they are and what they mean, refer to your drone's user manual.

Typically, before you can get airborne, you must arm your drone's flight controller and motors. The process for doing this may differ from drone to drone, but the purpose is the same for every drone. Arming the drone is the last thing you do before you start flying. It tells the drone that it is go time and gives control to the controller. If your safety indicator indicates that your drone is armed, DO NOT PICK IT UP. An armed drone is ready to fly, and any movement can cause the propellers to automatically start spinning to try to stabilize the device. If you pick up an armed drone, you run the risk of injury from the propellers. Figure 6-4 is a picture of a safety indicator for a drone that is disarmed.

Whether you are getting ready to fly or you are wrapping up a flight, do not pick up your drone unless the device is clearly disarmed. For increased safety, disconnect the battery as well.

Figure 6-3:
Parrot's
protective
hull for
the AR 2.0
drone.

Source: Adam Meek/Creative Commons

Figure 6-4:
Drone
safety
indicators
should keep
you safe.

Source: Nan Palmero/Creative Commons

Reducing the Risk of Drone Crashes

Crashes are almost a guarantee with drone flying. There are so many causes for drone crashes that it is almost impossible to plan for and anticipate every scenario. There are, however, several things you can do to reduce the probability of a crash:

- ✔ **Know your environment:** Before you get airborne, be sure to scout the area. Look for towers, cables supporting vertical structures, trees, power lines, buildings, and other structures that may block your drone's flightpath.

- ✔ **Use a spotter:** If you are flying with a first person view device, consider using a spotter to watch your drone. A spotter is a second person that keeps an eye on your drone, sometimes with binoculars if you are flying at long distances. First person views are restricted to the view of the camera that is streaming your flight. A spotter can help keep you from danger as long as you remain in sight.

- ✔ **Use a level and stable take-off and landing location:** Your drone will automatically calibrate before taking off. Make sure you have a stable, level location for taking off and landing so that your drone can calibrate accurately.

- ✔ **Fly in good weather:** Good weather means no wind, mild temperatures, and no precipitation.

- ✔ **Battery life:** If your drone's battery is running low, you need to bring your drone home. If you don't think you have enough juice to bring it back, slowly bring the drone back to earth and then go pick up your drone.

Even if you take all of the items above into consideration, there are several other factors that can contribute to the loss of control of your drone and a subsequent crash such as random mechanical or computer failure, battery failure, unanticipated collision with wildlife, or a run-in with a zealous anti-drone advocate.

Vortex ring state

The air that is forced down through your propellers is called *downwash*. Figure 6-5 is a picture showing a helicopter's downwash on the surface of water. If your drone descends to quickly, it will descend into its downwash which will cause it to lose lift at an increasingly rapid pace. This condition is called a *vortex ring state,* and if it is not corrected quickly, your drone will come crashing down. You can avoid VRS simply by controlling your rate of descent. Refer to your user manual to learn a safe rate of descent for your particular drone.

GPS lock

Most drones today are equipped with GPS capabilities. Before you start flying, you should ensure your drone has a *GPS lock.* The GPS lock tells your drone where your take-off and landing location is using GPS coordinates. This is critical in case you lose connection with your drone, regardless of whether you lose connection because the drone is flying out of range or some other communication failure occurs. With the GPS lock set, the drone should return to the GPS locked location.

This feature is fantastic in the event you do lose communication with your drone. Without a GPS lock, the drone flies until it runs out of juice or collides with something.

Figure 6-5:
A heli-
copter's
downwash
is easy to
see on the
open water.

Source: Vicki Burton/Creative Commons

Be warned that some drones do not forget their GPS lock. This means that you must be sure to reset the GPS lock every time you fly your drone if you are flying in different locations. Otherwise if your drone goes out of range, it may try to return to a different location entirely because of the GPS lock.

The DJI Phantom had a known bug that would cause Phantoms to fly away upon arming. The device would think that it was out of range, and it would automatically take off in the direction of the previous GPS lock. Since the writing of this book, DJI has provided a software update to fix this bug, it's still a good idea to be aware of this in the event you're ever flying a drone that behaves in this manner.

You should never rely on a GPS lock; it is only a backup to be used in the event of an emergency.

Safely Handling Lithium Polymer Batteries

For the most part, the go-to battery used in drones is a *lithium polymer battery* (*LiPo* for short). Most LiPo batteries are not a true lithium polymer batteries but rather a hybrid between two battery technologies. First and foremost, batteries use chemical reactions to produce electricity. A true lithium polymer battery creates electricity with a chemical reaction between dry components. Unfortunately, this doesn't create electrical current at a rate that is necessary for drone motors. So drones use a hybrid battery that combines wet and dry chemicals to facilitate the reaction at the rate necessary to power high-energy consumers such as drones.

LiPo batteries are ideal for drones because they can be built in many shapes and sizes, they have a favorable size to power ratio, and they have a high energy discharge rate which is ideal for electric motors. But for all of their benefits for use in drones, LiPo batteries are still very dangerous if not cared for correctly.

Properly charging a LiPo battery

The most common way to damage a LiPo battery is by overcharging it. Overcharging a battery can cause your battery to swell like the one shown in Figure 6-6. Swollen batteries can catch fire and explode. Over-discharging your battery can also cause issues if it remains un-charged long enough. The battery chemicals can come out of solution and cause the battery to short when you attempt to charge it again. A LiPo battery that is shorting out internally can explode and catch fire.

Figure 6-6:
Bury
swollen LiPo
batteries
in a bucket
of sand.

Source: U.S. Navy photo by Photographer's Mate Airman Sarah E. Ard

Most drones come with proprietary battery shapes and connectors. This is probably more of a function of commerce than safety, but regardless, use only the charges designated for your drone's batteries. If you buy an aftermarket charger, be sure to read your drone's manual to ensure that your charger has all the proper safety mechanisms to ensure you never overcharge.

Never leave your battery on a charger if you don't intend to monitor its progress. If your charger's shutoff feature fails, you could end up with a problem on your hands.

Avoiding dropping or crashing your LiPo battery

LiPo batteries are also very fragile. So fragile that simply dropping a LiPo battery on the floor can damage a cell and cause the chemicals within the battery to react uncontrollably. If your drone is involved in a crash, you will want to ensure that the battery did not withstand any damage. Placing a damaged battery on the charger can result in a fire.

Safely disposing of LiPo batteries

LiPo batteries are typically considered to be beyond usable life once they degrade to about 20 percent of their original capacity. At this point, you should stop flying with the battery as it may fully discharge before you can safely land your drone.

LiPo batteries can't simply be thrown away in the garbage can. While they may not be fit to fly, they can still be quite dangerous. Before throwing your battery away, you must first completely discharge the electrical charge. Most chargers come with a discharge feature that will drain the power from the battery rendering it fit for the garbage can.

If your battery is damaged or swollen, you still need to discharge the battery before tossing it out. You should not put it back onto the charger to discharge it. A common way for discharging damaged LiPo batteries involves connecting it to a light bulb and burying the battery in a bucket of sand until it is fully discharged. The safest option, however, would be to take it to your local hobby shop and let the experts dispose of it. If you can't get to a hobby shop right away, put the damaged battery into a bucket of sand until you can get to one.

Chapter 7

Knowing the Law

• •

• •

The safety of airline passengers and commercial air travel has been first and foremost on everyone's mind since the tragic events of September 11, 2001. The FAA has worked with Congress to pass legislation to address new issues that arise as new technologies become more and more readily available to the general public. You may recall a news story or two involving laser pointers and passenger jets. Or if you've flown recently, you may have noticed that you can use electronics like phones and other handheld devices during taxi and takeoff, whereas in recent history, no electronics were allowed until the aircraft was above 10,000 feet.

The advancements in drone technology have allowed for rapid development and distribution of drones that are capable of technological feats that were once the subject of science fiction. As a result, the FAA and government agencies around the world have had to quickly roll out rules and systems to manage the influx of air traffic. In addition to simply managing air congestion, many people have expressed concerns regarding personal privacy issues, use by law enforcement, surveillance, and property rights.

The legal landscape is evolving, but it will take time to open the skies to everyone. In early 2015, the FAA rolled out new guidelines for commercial use of drones, but it wasn't reasonable enough to allow for mass adoption. Some organizations, including Amazon and a few movie studios, have gotten special dispensation, but these instances are determined on a case-by-case basis.

The goal of this chapter is to give you an understanding of what the law is and how that will impact where you can fly your drone, what you can use your drone for, and what to do in the event someone is using a drone in a manner that makes you uncomfortable. Last, you explore how other countries' rules regarding drone use differ from those in the United States. You may not realize it, but this is a historic moment in America as we set the foundation for how to further integrate advanced machines into our culture.

Know Before You Fly in the United States

Remote-controlled vehicles have been around for quite some time. As discussed in Chapter 1, remote-controlled aircraft were first developed for hobby flyers back in the 1940s and 1950s. As you can probably imagine, the technology required to fly these aircraft was limited. Duration of flight was short, the method of controlling the craft was archaic at best, and the cost to get into the hobby was prohibitive enough that there wasn't an immediate need to enact strict legislation to govern the use of model aircraft. This is no longer the case. The two main drivers in the growth of the hobby unmanned aircraft industry are advancements in battery technology and smartphone technology.

The new LiPo batteries hold more charge for a longer time and can output charge at a rate needed to power high-energy-consuming motors on modern drones. The other major advancement is smartphones and wireless communication protocols used therein. Long-range cellular connections, GPS, Bluetooth, and Wi-Fi have made it possible to change how unmanned aircraft are controlled. The advancements in technology and the decrease and cost have made it possible for more flight enthusiasts to get into the hobby. The dramatic increase in civil drone use has caused many questions to be raised that quite frankly are still unanswered. Questions like:

- Who is going to manage all of the additional air traffic and how will they manage it?
- How do we protect people and property underneath the air traffic from accidents?
- Big brother programs and government surveillance is already in question. How will we determine fair use by the government that does not violate constitutional rights?
- How will we re-define property rights, trespassing, and personal protection?
- How do you manage commercial use for unmanned systems?
- Who is going to insure all of these people?

Currently, the law is very precisely designed to cover use of antiquated hobby model aircraft. As a result, congress has mandated to the FAA that they produce a plan for integrating civil unmanned aircraft systems (UAS), or as we call them, drones, into the national airspace system. The plan is to be presented to Congress no later than September 30, 2015. Until the new plans are presented, approved, and implemented, drone usage is limited to the following:

✔ *Aircraft is flown specifically for hobby or recreational use only.*

Hobby or recreational use is generally understood to mean any use that is not resulting in compensation in any form. Using your drone for recreation, personal joy, taking photographs, videos, and so on is generally thought to be recreational or hobby use. Using your drone to perform a task on the job like inspecting structures; capturing video or photos for marketing or documentation; performing surveillance; working security; conducting environmental monitoring; or capturing video or photos that you intend to sell, would all be considered commercial uses and would likely be found to be in violation of law.

✔ *Aircraft is flown in accordance with community-based set of safety guidelines.*

Community-based safety guidelines are generally considered to be safety guidelines as set forth by the Academy of Model Aeronautics (AMA). A complete and updated listing of the rules can be found online at `www.modelaircraft.org/files/105.pdf`. The current rules are also shown in Figure 7-1.

✔ *The Aircraft must be under 55 lbs.*

The good news is that unless you custom built your drone or you have a lot of excess cash and purchased an extremely high-end Boeing aircraft, your drone should be nowhere close to violating this.

✔ *Aircraft does not interfere with manned aircraft.*

This is generally interpreted to mean that a drone can't come anywhere near a manned flight. Regardless if it is a private plane, commercial passenger flight, or anything else as long as there are people in the aircraft. This is also where the flight ceiling comes into play. Flying your drone in excess of 400 feet above the ground is considered illegal. This is largely due to the fact that commercial airspace tends to start around 400 feet above the ground and flying a drone above 400 feet would be deemed an interference with manned aircraft regardless if there is a manned aircraft in the vicinity of your drone. That said, "interference with manned aircraft" is relatively vague and would be left to a court to interpret in the event you were caught in violation and prosecuted.

Academy of Model Aeronautics National Model Aircraft Safety Code
Effective January 1, 2014

A. **GENERAL**: A model aircraft is a non-human-carrying aircraft capable of sustained flight in the atmosphere. It may not exceed limitations of this code and is intended exclusively for sport, recreation, education and/or competition. All model flights must be conducted in accordance with this safety code and any additional rules specific to the flying site.

1. Model aircraft will not be flown:
    (a) In a careless or reckless manner.
    (b) At a location where model aircraft activities are prohibited.
2. Model aircraft pilots will:
    (a) Yield the right of way to all human-carrying aircraft.
    (b) See and avoid all aircraft and a spotter must be used when appropriate. (AMA Document #540-D.)
    (c) Not fly higher than approximately 400 feet above ground level within three (3) miles of an airport without notifying the airport operator.
    (d) Not interfere with operations and traffic patterns at any airport, heliport or seaplane base except where there is a mixed use agreement.
    (e) Not exceed a takeoff weight, including fuel, of 55 pounds unless in compliance with the AMA Large Model Airplane program. (AMA Document 520-A.)
    (f) Ensure the aircraft is identified with the name and address or AMA number of the owner on the inside or affixed to the outside of the model aircraft. (This does not apply to model aircraft flown indoors.)
    (g) Not operate aircraft with metal-blade propellers or with gaseous boosts except for helicopters operated under the provisions of AMA Document #555.
    (h) Not operate model aircraft while under the influence of alcohol or while using any drug that could adversely affect the pilot's ability to safely control the model.
    (i) Not operate model aircraft carrying pyrotechnic devices that explode or burn, or any device which propels a projectile or drops any object that creates a hazard to persons or property.
        Exceptions:
        • Free Flight fuses or devices that burn producing smoke and are securely attached to the model aircraft during flight.
        • Rocket motors (using solid propellant) up to a G-series size may be used provided they remain attached to the model during flight. Model rockets may be flown in accordance with the National Model Rocketry Safety Code but may not be launched from model aircraft.
        • Officially designated AMA Air Show Teams (AST) are authorized to use devices and practices as defined within the Team AMA Program Document. (AMA Document #718.)
    (j) Not operate a turbine-powered aircraft, unless in compliance with the AMA turbine regulations. (AMA Document #510-A.)
3. Model aircraft will not be flown in AMA sanctioned events, air shows or model demonstrations unless:
    (a) The aircraft, control system and pilot skills have successfully demonstrated all maneuvers intended or anticipated prior to the specific event.
    (b) An inexperienced pilot is assisted by an experienced pilot.
4. When and where required by rule, helmets must be properly worn and fastened. They must be OSHA, DOT, ANSI, SNELL or NOCSAE approved or comply with comparable standards.

B. **RADIO CONTROL (RC)**
1. All pilots shall avoid flying directly over unprotected people, vessels, vehicles or structures and shall avoid endangerment of life and property of others.
2. A successful radio equipment ground-range check in accordance with manufacturer's recommendations will be completed before the first flight of a new or repaired model aircraft.
3. At all flying sites a safety line(s) must be established in front of which all flying takes place. (AMA Document #706.)
    (a) Only personnel associated with flying the model aircraft are allowed at or in front of the safety line.
    (b) At air shows or demonstrations, a straight safety line must be established.
    (c) An area away from the safety line must be maintained for spectators.
    (d) Intentional flying behind the safety line is prohibited.
4. RC model aircraft must use the radio-control frequencies currently allowed by the Federal Communications Commission (FCC). Only individuals properly licensed by the FCC are authorized to operate equipment on Amateur Band frequencies.
5. RC model aircraft will not knowingly operate within three (3) miles of any pre-existing flying site without a frequency-management agreement. (AMA Documents #922 and #923.)
6. With the exception of events flown under official AMA Competition Regulations, excluding takeoff and landing, no powered model may be flown outdoors closer than 25 feet to any individual, except for the pilot and the pilot's helper(s) located at the flightline.
7. Under no circumstances may a pilot or other person touch an outdoor model aircraft in flight while it is still under power, except to divert it from striking an individual.
8. RC night flying requires a lighting system providing the pilot with a clear view of the model's attitude and orientation at all times. Hand-held illumination systems are inadequate for night flying operations.
9. The pilot of an RC model aircraft shall:
    (a) Maintain control during the entire flight, maintaining visual contact without enhancement other than by corrective lenses prescribed for the pilot.
    (b) Fly using the assistance of a camera or First-Person View (FPV) only in accordance with the procedures outlined in AMA Document #550.
    (c) Fly using the assistance of autopilot or stabilization system only in accordance with the procedures outlined in AMA Document #560.

C. **FREE FLIGHT**
1. Must be at least 100 feet downwind of spectators and automobile parking when the model aircraft is launched.
2. Launch area must be clear of all individuals except mechanics, officials, and other fliers.
3. An effective device will be used to extinguish any fuse on the model aircraft after the fuse has completed its function.

D. **CONTROL LINE**
1. The complete control system (including the safety thong where applicable) must have an inspection and pull test prior to flying.
2. The pull test will be in accordance with the current Competition Regulations for the applicable model aircraft category.
3. Model aircraft not fitting a specific category shall use those pull-test requirements as indicated for Control Line Precision Aerobatics.
4. The flying area must be clear of all utility wires or poles and a model aircraft will not be flown closer than 50 feet to any above-ground electric utility lines.
5. The flying area must be clear of all nonessential participants and spectators before the engine is started.

Courtesy of Mark LaFay

Figure 7-1:
AMA's community flying safety guidelines.

↳ *The Aircraft is not flown within 5 miles of an airport unless cleared beforehand with the Air Traffic Control (ATC).*

The AMA rules of safety say that you cannot fly within 3 miles of an airport unless you have prior clearance. In this case the FAA's ruling would prevail so as a rule of thumb, flying within 5 miles of an airport without clearance should be considered a major no-no. While the law says that you can get clearance from the air traffic control, the likelihood of this being granted is slim-to-none. Therefore, stay away from the airports. This may not sound like a difficult task but the map in Figure 7-2 shows a radius of the different airports in the Indianapolis area. Notice the radius of each airport and how much of the airspace above Indianapolis is restricted.

↳ *The Aircraft is flown within line of sight of the operator.*

Flying within line of sight means that you can see your aircraft at all times while it is airborne. Until recently, hobby model aircraft flyers were restricted to flying in line of site simply because that is all that the technology would allow. With today's drones you can fly line of sight, or you can use GPS tracking, first person video feeds, and other advanced autopilot modes to fly your drone well beyond the restriction of line-of-sight. Current laws make this method of flight, illegal. Figure 7-3 shows a tablet that has several GPS beacons indicated for a drone's flight path. As long as the drone remains within eyeshot, this is legal.

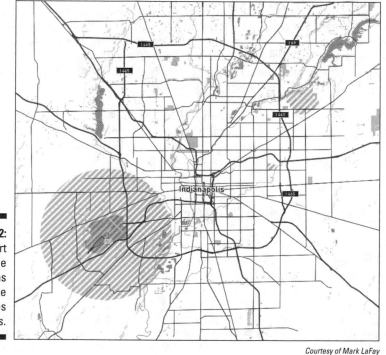

Figure 7-2: Airport airspace restrictions can make entire cities no-fly zones.

Courtesy of Mark LaFay

Figure 7-3:
GPS flight
mode is
legal if you
can see
your drone
at all times.

No-fly zones

In addition to the rules set forth by the FAA, there are regulations that have restricted drone flight near or over government buildings, in national parks, and anywhere near military installations. Also, due to the concentration of government facilities, personnel, airports, and military bases, flying a drone in or around Washington D.C. is a bad idea — if you are caught, you will likely be prosecuted swiftly. In late January of 2015, a government employee was in a lot of hot water for not only flying a drone while under the influence of alcohol (a big no-no according to the AMA safety guidelines), but he crashed his DJI Phantom on the lawn of the White House. The official statement was that he was intending to prove that the aerial alert system at the White House was inadequate and needed to be upgraded. He was right, but time will tell if he will get a promotion at work or jail time.

To stay up-to-date on no-fly zones in the United States, check out the website https://www.mapbox.com/blog/dont-fly-here, shown in Figure 7-4. This site has an interactive map that is community updated. It shows where you can and can't fly your drone in the U.S.

State and local laws

In 2014, a total of 35 states had begun considering legislation impacting Unmanned Aircraft Systems (UAS) but only ten have actually enacted the laws. Although your city or state may not have enacted laws governing the use of drones, that doesn't mean that you won't get some grief from law enforcement anyway. Police Chief Robert Marshall of Naperville, Illinois, began a legal inquiry to determine if the city could arrest and prosecute a drone pilot for taking video and photos of the city of Naperville at night. Below is a listing of states that have enacted UAS (drone) legislation along with a summary of the legislation and the Bill identification:

Don't fly drones here

By 🐦 Bobby Sudekum on July 22 2014

Unmanned drones like quadcopters and fixed-wing aircraft are at the center of new airspace regulations by the FAA. While the FAA deliberates on rules and regulations, states, cities and other national organizations have implemented their own no-fly zones. To help people find safe places to fly, we've mapped established no-fly areas where drones are not permitted around all major airports, military bases, and national parks across the country. All the no-fly area data we collected to make these maps is now open data under CC-0. *Go explore the map*

Figure 7-4: MapBox website shows the no-fly zones in the U.S. on an interactive map.

Courtesy of Mark LaFay

- ✔ **Alaska:** Bill HB255

   This bill outlines procedures and standards for law enforcement use of unmanned aircraft. The bill requires law enforcement to get FAA authorization to use the aircraft for all activities. It also requires a law enforcement to have a search warrant to use a drone to search private property.

- ✔ **Illinois:** Bill SB2937

   This bill created regulations for how law enforcement can obtain and use information gathered using unmanned aircraft. It also loosens regulations regarding how law enforcement uses unmanned aircraft during disasters and public health emergencies.

- ✔ **Indiana:** Bill HB1009

   This bill outlines warrant requirements and exceptions for police use of drones. It also enacted a new law that created the crime of "Unlawful Photography and Surveillance on Private Property," which makes it a Class A misdemeanor to knowingly and intentionally survey private property without permission.

- **Iowa:** Bill HF 2289

  This bill makes it illegal for a state agency to use a drone to enforce traffic laws. The new law also requires a warrant, to gather information with a drone and later use the information in a civil or criminal court proceeding.

- **Louisiana:** Bill HB1029

  This bill created the new crime of "Unlawful use of an unmanned aircraft system," which defines the unlawful use of an unmanned aircraft system as the intentional use of a drone to survey a targeted facility without the owner's prior written consent. The crime is punishable by fine and imprisonment.

- **North Carolina:** Bill SB744

  This bill prohibits anyone from conducting drone surveillance of a person or private property and also prohibits taking a photo of a person without their consent for the purpose of distributing it. The bill also authorizes commercial use of drones for agriculture, mapping, research, and forest management. Law enforcement can use drones to monitor public spaces and counteract terrorism as long as a warrant is secured. The bill also created several new crimes: using UAS to interfere with manned aircraft, possessing an unmanned aircraft with an attached weapon, the unlawful fishing or hunting with an unmanned aircraft, harassing hunters or fisherman with an unmanned aircraft, unlawful distribution of images obtained with an unmanned aircraft, and operating an unmanned aircraft commercially without a license.

- **Ohio:** Bill HB292

  This bill created Ohio's aerospace and aviation technology committee. One of their duties is to research and develop aviation technology including unmanned aerial vehicles.

- **Tennessee:** Bill SB1777

  This bill makes it illegal to conduct surveillance on anyone that is hunting or fishing. Bill SB1777 makes it a crime to conduct surveillance of an individual or their property, to possesses surveillance photos or video footage, or to distribute those photos or videos. The bill also outlines legal commercial uses for unmanned aircraft.

- **Utah:** Bill SB167

  This bill requires law enforcement to acquire a warrant in order to use a drone to "obtain, receive or use data."

✔ **Wisconsin:** Bill SB196

> This bill requires law enforcement to obtain a warrant before using
> drones in a place where an individual has a "reasonable expectation
> of privacy" like your home. The law also created a new law to prevent
> weaponization of drones and another law to prevent the use of a drone
> to observe another individual in a place where they have a "reasonable
> expectation of privacy."

As you probably noticed, there were several laws enacted to protect the
people from improper an unfair use by law enforcement. Some states are also
implementing laws to protect the general public from twenty-first century
peeping toms and other generally annoying and potentially unsafe behavior.

Multiple states have legislation on the docket for addressing the use of
drones to disrupt hunting and fishing. This is gaining momentum as animal
rights advocacy groups like PETA continue to encourage animal rights
activists to use drones to harass lawful hunting and fishing. Figure 7-5 shows
a picture of the PETA air angel.

Stay up-to-date on which states are doing what by checking the American
Civil Liberties Union website here: https://www.aclu.org/blog/
technology-and-liberty/status-2014-domestic-drone-
legislation-states

Figure 7-5:
PETA's air
angel is
designed
to disrupt
hunting.

Courtesy of Peta

Taking Matters Into Your Own Hands

Drones are definitely controversial largely due to the general public's perception of them as a tool for the government surveillance and other violations of personal civil liberties. The government's expansion of domestic use of drones for surveillance has caused many people to raise concerns, so much so that the ACLU has stepped in and recommended the following list of safe guards (that can also be found on their website, https://www.aclu.org/issues/privacy-technology/surveillance-technologies/domestic-drones?redirect=blog/tag/domestic-drones):

- ✔ **Usage limits:** Drones should be deployed by law enforcement only with a warrant, in an emergency, or when there are specific and articulable grounds to believe that the drone will collect evidence relating to a specific criminal act.

- ✔ **Data retention:** Images should be retained only when there is reasonable suspicion that they contain evidence of a crime or are relevant to an ongoing investigation or trial.

- ✔ **Policy:** Usage policy on domestic drones should be decided by the public's representatives, not by police departments, and the policies should be clear, written, and open to the public.

- ✔ **Abuse prevention & accountability:** Use of domestic drones should be subject to open audits and proper oversight to prevent misuse.

- ✔ **Weapons:** Domestic drones should not be equipped with lethal or non-lethal weapons.

For some, however, things aren't moving fast enough and so they've opted to take matters into their own hands. In 2013, the town of Deer Trail, Colorado, considered an ordinance that would pay a bounty for every drone shot out of the sky. This was not passed, but the proposal elevated the conversation on domestic surveillance with drones and ethical and legal boundaries for domestic drone usage, civil, commercial, and public.

In 2014, a New Jersey man was arrested for shooting a drone out of the sky with a shotgun. He felt the drone was invading his property and therefore defended his home from the invasion. He was, however, arrested for 2 gun-related crimes and the drone operator was not charged simply because there were no laws on the books preventing the use of his drone over his neighbor's property.

The home owner that took matters into his own hands argued that the drone was on private property; unfortunately, case law precedent said otherwise. In a 1946 Supreme Court decision U.S. vs. Causby, it was ruled that airspace is public highway and that airplanes could fly through it unencumbered by property law. Later in the 1980s, the Supreme Court also found that law enforcement didn't need a warrant for aerial images and that home owners did not have any expectation of privacy. In fact, if you were to damage someone else's drone, even if it was flying over your property, you could be found by a court to owe damages to repair or replace the drone. If someone parked their car on your lawn, you couldn't set it on fire, but you could have it towed and then sue the owner for any costs associated with the towing and repair to any damages to your lawn.

If you find that someone is invading your privacy with a drone and you want to take matters into your own hands, your best bet is to start with contacting law enforcement. The next step is to put your vote to work. Contact your state representatives. If you don't know who your federal representatives are, you can find out by visiting sites like: `https://www.opencongress.org/people/zipcodelookup`. If you want to know who your state-level representatives are, go to your state government's homepage.

Knowing the Laws in Other Countries

Generally speaking, the world tends to follow the lead of the FAA. Simply put, this is because if you want to fly into the US, you have to abide by the FAA's rules and regulations for the safe operation of an aircraft. The FAA's rules and regulations are typically regarded as rigorous. They should be; that is what ensures the safety of the millions of people who fly in and out of the United States every day. Laws regulating drones do, however, differ from country to country because, for the time being, no unmanned aircraft are being flown between sovereign nations. So if you are going to another country with your drone, you should get familiar with the country's laws so you don't end up the star of an episode of *Locked Up Abroad*. Below is a list of countries and a brief summary of their laws as well as a link to online resources:

- **Canada:** The laws in Canada are pretty strict when it comes to flying a drone legally. If you are using your drone for personal and recreational use, the drone is under 77 pounds, and you are absolutely not using it to make money, then the drone is considered a model aircraft. Anything else requires a special certification. Good luck! Here is a link to more information:

- **United Kingdom:** The laws in the UK are very similar to the U.S. Your drone needs to be under 20kg, you can't fly it for commercial purposes so no business functions or revenue generation with your drone without certification. You also need to fly line-of-sight, away from congested areas, and no higher than 400 feet above the ground. Also, similarly to the United States, there is criminal code that likely comes into play with privacy issues, trespassing, and such that you will want to be aware of. For more information:

✔ **Europe:** For most aviation-related topics, Europe is governed by European Aviation Safety Administration (EASA), however for remotely piloted systems (drones), they relegate responsibilities to each country in the European Union.

Part III
Miracle of Flight

In This Part . . .

- ✔ Controlling your drone
- ✔ Understanding flight basics
- ✔ Choosing a location to fly
- ✔ Performing maintenance on your drone

Chapter 8

Controlling Your Drone

In This Chapter

▶ Understanding how drones are piloted

▶ Controlling your drone

▶ Auto-piloting your drone

Getting your drone airborne and flying it with great skill requires more than just a deft hand, it requires high technology! The greatest technology innovation to drive the growth of the modern drone market is smartphones. Modern smartphones contain all of the advanced communication protocols that are necessary for drone flight. The Apple iPhone, and numerous Android devices, has a cellular radio which utilizes several long-range and short ranges frequencies. The iPhone also has wireless internet capabilities with Wi-Fi, Bluetooth, and global positioning service (GPS). Your iPhone also contains advanced sensors like temperature gauges, gyroscopes that determine the orientation of the phone, accelerometers that detect motion of the phone and can even detect acceleration. The smartphone industry not only drove the development and improvement of these technologies but also the miniaturization of these technologies.

Small and powerful are the words that should be used to describe the technology needed to get your drone into the sky. In this chapter, you will explore all of the different technologies that control your drone and keep it airborne. Learn how they all work together to give you directional control with a number of different devices like smartphones, tablets, and the tried and true radio controller.

Flying an aerial vehicle that can move in all directions requires advanced navigational skill. This chapter describes the difference in directional controls from heads-free to standard. Get a handle on how to steer your drone like a pro! Last, this chapter explores different advanced flying modes and autopilots that can make it easier for you to capture fantastic video and photos. Some modes are device-specific, and some are universal. Take a look at how you can use these advanced flying modes to make your drone flying experience the best.

Understanding How Your Drone Is Controlled

Hobbyists have been flying remote-controlled aircraft since the 1940s. For the most part, the aircraft have been nothing more than airplanes with motors. The technology needed to get an airplane airborne and to control it remotely is far less complex than what is necessary for a multi-rotor aircraft, which is the popular aircraft of today. There are several reasons for this and it is largely due to the manner in which both aircraft get airborne. For an object that is heavier-than-air to get airborne, you must create lift. *Lift* is a force that pushes an object upward into the air and is created by varying the air pressure above and below an aircraft.

Airplanes create lift by moving air above and below a wing (and around the plane). The way that air movement is created is with the horizontal movement of the aircraft. Think of airplanes taking off at an airport: the larger the aircraft, the longer the runway they need to gain the right amount of speed to create the lift that will ultimately push the aircraft into the air. Once airborne, the aircraft must maintain horizontal momentum in order to keep the right amount of air moving over the wings. Figure 8-1 shows an aircraft that is airborne. The aircraft moves only in the direction that the nose is pointing. That

Figure 8-1:
Directional
control
requires
constant
forward
movement.

Source: NASA/Tom Tschida

means that side to side, reverse, and vertical movement are not a possibility for airplanes.

Helicopters and multi-rotors achieve lift by the same principles as an airplane, only they create lift by drawing air down through their propellers at a high rate of speed. This creates lift on the propellers which push the craft directly upward. With helicopters, directional control is achieved by changing the direction in which the propellers lean, by changing the pitch of the blades. This is called *changing the attack* of the propellers. Helicopters typically only have one main propeller but multi-rotors have more than one.

The most popular drones available today are multi-rotors with at least three propellers and some have in upwards of eight propellers. Multi-rotors maintain stability by varying the speeds of each propeller. Directional control in a drone is achieved by changing the attack of the propellers, the same as a helicopter, but this change in attack is accomplished by slowing some of the rotors to cause the craft angle to change enough to cause it to move. Figure 8-2 shows the directional capabilities of a multi-rotor aircraft, a style that is common for modern drones. As shown in Figure 8-2, multi-rotor aircraft have the benefit of 3-dimensional movement where as an airplane is limited to planar movement.

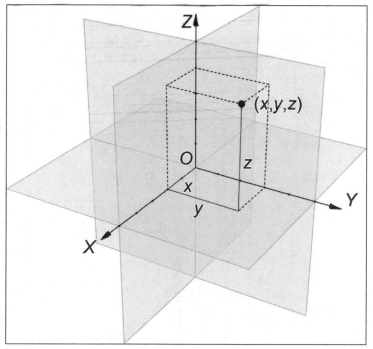

Figure 8-2:
Rotocraft are capable of 3-dimensional movement.

Credit: Source: Jorge Stolfi

The benefit to flying an airplane over a rotorcraft is that it requires substantially less power, and fuel, to get an airplane in the air. Airplanes can move at faster speeds, over greater distances for longer periods of time than a helicopters.

For a multi-rotor drone, there are two advanced sensors that are required to be able to achieve steady 3-dimensional flight:

- ✔ **Accelerometer:** These advanced sensors detect linear movement. That means movement in a straight line. There are three axes in a 3D space: X, Y, and Z. Accelerometers detect and measure movement along those axes but not around. This movement is called *linear movement*. Anything other than linear movement confuses an accelerometer. Figure 8-3 is a picture of linear movement along an axis.

- ✔ **Gyroscope:** This sensor is designed to detect rotational movement. That means movement around a line which, in a 3D space, are the X, Y, and Z axes. Whereas an accelerometer measures motion along the axis, a gyroscope will measure motion around an axis. Figure 8-3 shows an illustration of gyroscopic movement.

Gyros, short for "gyroscopes," and accelerometers are necessary for maintaining stability and flight control. If you can't detect the orientation of your drone, you won't be able to maintain flight and then everything will come crashing down.

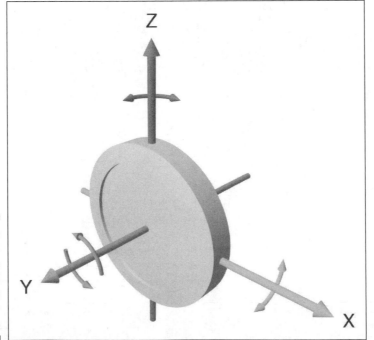

Figure 8-3:
3D movement is detected with gyros and accelerometers.

Source: LucasVB/Creative Commons

Radio Frequency

In order to control a drone remotely, you must be able to communicate with it wirelessly. That means you want to be able to send it directional information without needing to be physically connected to the drone by a cable. Since the early days of remote control flying, this wireless navigation was achieved using radio waves. Radio waves are an invisible wave form on the electromagnetic spectrum. Like all things on the electromagnetic spectrum, radio is measured in hertz (Hz). Extremely low frequency is anywhere from 3Hz to 30Hz and tremendously high frequency is 300 GHz – 3000GHz.

A great example of radio frequency (RF) communication is a common audio radio. Audible content is transmitted wirelessly over long distances using radio transmitting towers. Your radio receiver then picks up the waves and translates them into the audio that comes out of the speakers. FM radio is between 90MHz and 110MHz. For radio to work, you must have a transmitter to send the messages and a receiver to get the messages. At a rudimentary level, this is how remotely controlling an aircraft is accomplished. More precisely, your transmitter and receiver need to be tuned to the same frequency; otherwise, they won't be able to connect and send directional information.

Here is where it might get a little confusing. Radio frequency is just a method for communicating. There are billions of devices around the globe that communicate using wireless communication in the RF segment of the electromagnetic spectrum. These radio transmissions are always present everywhere you go in the world. You just have to have a receiver that is capable of fine-tuning to the correct frequency to receive it. To avoid situations such as your drone being controlled by someone else's remote control, devices use a unique identification code to identify a transmission on one particular radio frequency as the transmission it wants to receive. To do this, transmitters and receivers are paired using an RFID or a "radio frequency identification." All information broadcast over RFID is prefixed with an RFID so that the receiver knows that the information it is picking up is for it.

Lower frequencies tend to have a much greater range at lower power than higher frequency devices. Lower frequencies also have a greater ability to penetrate dense objects which is another reason why they are great for remote controlling a drone. However, the lower the frequency, the larger the antenna must be to receive the frequency. Most remote control drones use 900 MHz for transmission. Higher frequencies in the 2.4 GHz range are predominantly used for Wi-Fi, which you will learn about below. Figure 8-4 is a picture of the RF controller that the DJI Phantom 2 uses.

Figure 8-4:
The DJI
Phantom
2 remote
control uses
RF.

Wi-Fi Controls

The Wi-Fi alliance says that Wi-Fi is any "wireless local area network" product based on the Institute of Electrical and Electronics Engineers (IEEE) standard 802.11. Today, Wi-Fi is used universally to mean a wireless means to connect to the Internet. Wi-Fi used to only be available on computers but as the technology evolved, shrunk, and grew more intelligent, it was integrated into portable devices like phones and tablets. Now there are several million products around the world that are Wi-Fi-enabled so that they can be remotely accessible.

Most drones today are Wi-Fi enabled so that they can broadcast video to a computer, tablet, or smartphone. Some drones also use Wi-Fi for remote controlling through a tablet or mobile application. The Parrot AR Drone 2.0 offers high-end interactive controls with their mobile application that runs on an iPhone or iPad. Figure 8-5 is a picture of the Parrot AR Drone 2.0 tablet controls.

While there are clear benefits to using Wi-Fi to control your drone or simply communicate information back from your drone like environmental data, video, or photos, Wi-Fi works on an ultra high radio frequency which means that its range is limited to about 600 meters.

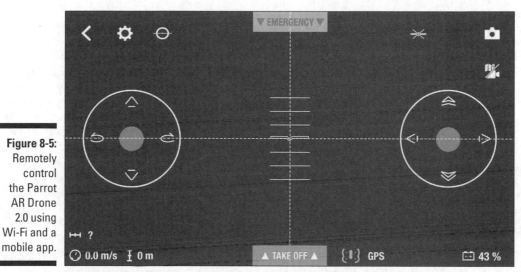

Figure 8-5:
Remotely
control
the Parrot
AR Drone
2.0 using
Wi-Fi and a
mobile app.

Courtesy of Andrew Amato

GPS

Global positioning technology has shrunk down enough that it is possible to
ping satellites for location data from devices as small as a smartphone and your
drone. GPS is primarily only used to communicate location back to a mobile
app. GPS is also used for pre-programming routes. For example the DJI Phantom
2 gives you the ability to program a route with several GPS coordinates. Once
programmed, the drone can be cut loose and it will fly in sequence to each of
the GPS locations identified. Figure 8-6 is a picture of the DJI interactive map
where a user can specify a flight route with GPS coordinates.

Figure 8-6:
Plot a route
with GPS
and then
set it and
forget it!

Courtesy of Andrew Amato

Directional Control

Becoming an expert level drone pilot requires a little extra flight training. By design, multi-rotor aircraft have great navigational control, but that control takes time to master. Airplanes, unlike multi-rotor aircraft, can only fly nose forward which means that if you want to go a particular direction, you need to steer that direction much like you would in a boat. Quadcopters, however, have the ability to go forward and backward, move left and right, and move vertically. Directional control is achieved by adjusting the roll, pitch, yaw, and throttle of your quadcopter.

- ✔ **Roll:** Tilts your quadcopter to the left or the right by speeding up the rotors on one side of your quadcopter and slowing them down on the other side. By doing so, one side of the drone will sag, or tilt downward, causing the drone to strafe to the left or the right.

- ✔ **Pitch:** Tilts your quadcopter forward and backward in the same manner as rolling. By adjusting the pitch, your drone will sag down in the front causing it to go forward, or sag in the back causing it to go backwards.

- ✔ **Yaw:** Rotates the nose of your aircraft left to right. Quadcopter propellers do not tall spin in the same direction. If they did, the centrifugal force would cause them to just spin out of control. In order to combat that, diagonally opposing propellers spin in the same direction. Figure 8-7 is a picture detailing the directions in which propellers spin. To rotate your quadcopter the rotors that spin in the same direction will speed up to rotate the air craft to the left or the right.

- ✔ **Throttle:** Controls the motion of your drone up and down by speeding up or slowing down all of the propellers.

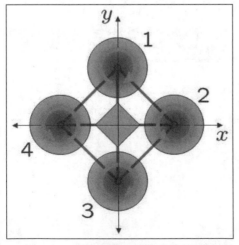

Figure 8-7:
Propellers
do not all
spin the
same
direction.

Source: Grabriel Hoffmann/ Creative Commons.

Standard Mode

There are several different names and terms to refer to the different flight modes for your drone. Standard mode, also known as Normal mode (and other names), is the most common flight mode. And probably the safest for new pilots. To put it simply, standard mode controls function as if you were sitting in the cockpit piloting the control. The controls are relative to the front of the drone. Inexperienced pilots can get into trouble in this mode because when the drone is facing the pilot, the controls can seem to be reversed. Just remind yourself that you are always flying from the perspective of being in the pilot seat.

Heads Free Mode

When your drone is in Heads Free mode, also known as *Simple mode* or *Carefree mode,* your controls are set based on the orientation of the drone when it was armed. For example, if your drone was facing north and you were standing behind it, forward will always send it north, backward will always send it south; the same goes for the side to sides. This can be somewhat confusing, but it can come in handy in the event your drone is ever far enough away that you can't determine the direction it is pointing (heading).

First Person View

First person view (FPV) is a new flight mode for consumer drone fliers. In FPV mode, the pilot is able to fly using the onboard cameras acting as his eyes. The camera is typically a narrow focus, front-facing camera, giving the pilot the ability to pilot the craft as if he were onboard and behind the controls. In order to fly in FPV mode, your drone must come with a front-facing camera. Your drone must also have the option for live streaming the video feed to a display device. This almost always requires a Wi-Fi connection which then places a restriction on the distance you can fly in FPV mode to about 600 meters or less.

The FAA hasn't placed an official ban on FPV flying, but the law specifically says that if you are hobby flying, you must fly line-of-sight. That said, if your drone offers FPV flight mode and you want to limit your risk of potentially getting busted, you should fly out in the middle of nowhere. Figure 8-8 shows the view from a DJI drone with a FPV control setup.

Figure 8-8:
First person
view is a fun
flight mode.

Other Flight Modes and Autopilots

There are several different modes in which you can fly your drone aside from the more common modes like *standard* and *heads free*. Unfortunately, there isn't a standard set of terms for how to describe the different modes, and so one vendor may call it one thing and another vendor will call it something totally different. For example, GPS lock mode is also referred to as loiter mode. Following is a list of other flight modes and some autopilot modes

- ✔ **Altitude Hold mode:** In this mode, your drone's current altitude will be maintained. Roll, pitch, and yaw will operate the same, but the altitude will remain constant.

- ✔ **Loiter mode:** In this mode, your drone will automatically maintain your location, heading (where you are headed), and altitude even after your hands have been taken off the control sticks. The pilot can fly loiter mode as if it is in a manual mode, but you don't have to worry about a crash if you take your fingers off the sticks mistakenly.

- ✔ **Stabilize mode:** This mode allows you to fly your drone manually. The drone will automatically level out after you make directional corrections, however. When you roll or pitch a drone, it causes the drone to lean the device in order to move in that direction. In a fully manual mode, you would have to level out the pitch or roll manually. Stabilize mode does this automatically.

✔ **Auto Return mode:** Numerous drones offer a feature that will cause your drone to fly back to the place where it was armed in the event that control communication is lost. This feature is usually initialized by default, but refer to your manual to ensure that it is; otherwise, you could lose your drone if you get out of range or lose battery power in your controller.

Chapter 9

Flight Basics

. . . .

. . . .

*T*his chapter is about firing up your drone, taking to the skies, and seeing the world from a vantage point that until now was reserved for the birds. In this chapter, you explore the steps that lead directly to flight. For good measure, you should review the later chapters about where and when to fly and how to take great photos and videos with your drone camera before you get going. But if you simply can't wait, then at least promise yourself to finish the book at some point! If you don't finish he book, you'll miss out on a lot of helpful information that could speed you along on your path to being an expert drone flyer and aerial photographer. You'll also miss out on some good ideas about how to use your drone for business!

Use this chapter to build a list of things you always do before you power up and get vertical. Get a brief look under the hood to understand what happens when your drone calibrates before flight. Get comfortable with the limits of your drone so that you can operate well within them. Estimate your drone's range of flight and understand what can impact that range. Get to know how to understand what your drone is telling you regardless if you are using a mobile app on a tablet or smartphone or using the handheld remote control. Last, see how to plan for anomalies during flight and learn how to land safely under normal circumstances and in the case of an emergency.

Pre-Flight Checklist

When I was a kid, we took many family vacations that involved flying. In fact, I flew by myself a few times, or with my brother who is two years older than I am. I remember being on numerous flights when the cockpit door would actually be open during flight. Getting on the plane, sometimes my brother and I would dawdle up by the cockpit just to look at all of the lights, dials, switches, buttons, and flashy things. Every once in a while, the pilots would let us come up into the cockpit when they were getting ready to fly. I distinctly remember watching the pilot and first officer or co-pilot going through their checklists of things that they need to do before pushing back from the gate and taxiing onto the runway. The checklist was their guideline for ensuring a safe flight. You can imagine that it would be an exhaustive list!

Flying a drone is not as critical a task as flying a commercial airplane filled with people, but there are several things that need to be done to ensure that you have a successful flight free of harm to you, others, and your drone. To do this, you need to assemble a pre-flight checklist. Your checklist should include every last task no matter how mundane it seems and the list should be linear in nature. Meaning, *A* must occur before *B*. Figure 9-1 is a picture of a sample pre-flight checklist.

Your checklist should serve as a step-by-step reminder of all that you need to verify before you get airborne. The list is designed to keep you safe, keep others safe, and ensure the best flying experience possible. There is nothing worse than committing a day to flying and then blowing the day because you didn't plan appropriately.

Pre-Flight Checklist

Flight Date: _____

Flight Location: _____

Weather Conditions: _____

Check?	Item	Notes
	Is the location clear of people, power lines, and other objects?	
	Are you in a no fly zone?	
	Inspect Equipment for damage	
	First Aid Kit available?	
	Extra Batteries?	
	Verify Battery Charge Level	
	Place drone in a safe level location	
	Turn on camera	
	Verify Transmitter controls move	
	Verify transmitter controls in neutral position	
	Verify transmitter throttle to zero	
	Turn on transmitter	
	connect drone battery	
	Power on Drone	
	Start flight timer	
	Check for nearrby people and animals	
	Stand clear and announce "CLEAR"	
	Arm flight controller	
	Increase throttle slightly and check for abnormalities	
	Hover at 3-5 feet for a few seconds to check stability	

Figure 9-1:
Pre-flight checklists are different for each pilot and drone.

Courtesy of Mark LaFay

There are several types of drones on the market, so your list may be specific to your drone and technology configuration. However, the following sections detail a sample of things that should be considered for your own pre-flight checklist.

Environment

When you arrive at your flight location, ensure that you are aware of all of the obstacles in the area. This could include trees and other greenery, as well as towers, power lines, roads, water sources, buildings, and people. Regardless of the mode in which you intend to fly, you need to know what you need to navigate around, if anything.

No-fly zone

If you are near a major metro area, chances are good that you could be within five miles of an airport. You definitely don't want to fly your drone in this area because it is illegal.

Current laws say that if you have clearance from the air traffic controller, you can fly, but the chances are slim that you will either get through to them or get clearance to fly.

You can verify no-fly zone space by using mapping software on your smartphone, or you can go to www.mapbox.com/drone/no-fly. If you have a newer DJI drone, chances are good that it will automatically check to see if you are in a known no-fly zone. If you are in a known no-fly zone, the drone will not allow you to get airborne.

 The FAA keeps an updates list of no-fly zones and the list is sure to change in the near future. Stay up-to-date by checking the FAA's website. A good rule of thumb is to not fly within 5 miles of airports, in or near state or federal property (city parks included), and avoid schools and school property unless you have explicit permission.

Equipment spot check

This list varies in length depending on the gear you use to fly your drone. Regardless of the length of your gear list, don't shy away from listing everything down to the seemingly insignificant detail.

- Drone
- Drone case
- Battery charging station
- Transmitter
- Spare equipment
- Power chords
- Power strips
- Gimbal
- Camera
- Media cards
- Computer
- Media card readers
- Tablets
- Phones
- Safety gear like cones and flags
- Flight log
- Landing pad (if you bring one)

In your list, plan to check off that you have the item when you arrive and again when you pack up to leave (more on post-flight checklists in Chapter 11).

First Aid Kit

Verify not only that you have a first aid kit but that it has all of the necessary equipment in it. Bandages, triple antibiotic ointment, alcohol wipes, aspirin or Tylenol, and other basic gear is important. You also should consider packing several ace bandages, bandage tape, and even a tourniquet. You may be wondering why you would need a tourniquet and the answer is simple: propeller injuries can be nasty and if you get cut in a critical place, a tourniquet could be critical for stopping bleeding until you can get serious help. Remember the Boy Scout motto: Always be prepared. Of course, if your drone is extremely small, like the size of a softball, you don't have to worry about losing an arm or bleeding out. But careless behavior with even the tiniest of drones can result in some minor scrapes and scratches.

Batteries

If you have multiple batteries for your drone, be sure to number them and refer to them by their number. This avoids any confusion when you charge and swap out your batteries. Inspect your batteries before each use to ensure no physical damage has occurred to the battery or wires. Ensure that no swelling or bloating of the battery has occurred. Plug the batteries in to verify that they are at the proper charge level. If they need to be charged, you need to get this process started.

Inspection

Before every flight, you must review your drone. Check for physical breaks in the structure of the drone. Carefully review the landing gear, as well. If the landing gear is retractable, you want to make sure that all of the motorized gear is free of any visual flaws or defects.

Check for foreign matter that might gunk up the moving parts. Inspect all wiring for cuts or burns, and check that all physical wiring connections and harnesses are intact and connected. If your drone batteries slide into a special port, as they do with the DJI phantom drones, then you want to make sure there is no corrosion or other material that might interfere with making a proper connection.

Last, take a good look at your propellers and search for any damage whatsoever. Propellers are carefully balanced to ensure the stability of your drone during flight. Even a small scratch can throw off the balance of a single prop and that could make the entire drone become less stable. Figure 9-2 shows propellers that are slightly damaged and completely unusable.

 If you are in doubt of whether or not your propeller is damaged, replace it. Props are cheap especially in comparison to your drone as a whole (camera included). You can always take your prop to a hobby shop to have them inspect it if you aren't sure.

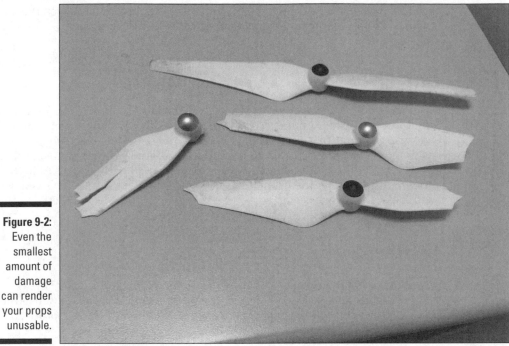

Courtesy of Andrew Amato

Figure 9-2:
Even the smallest amount of damage can render your props unusable.

Transmitter and ground station

Check your transmitter to make sure you have charged batteries and battery backups. Inspect the transmitter to ensure that your control sticks can move in all directions before setting them in the neutral positions (not stuck in any one direction). Ensure that your throttle is set to zero. If you have any other ground control equipment, make sure it is all properly connected and powered.

Camera gear

If you are flying with camera gear, ensure that the gear is properly attached to your drone. Verify that your camera batteries are properly charged and backups are ready. Clear all media cards to make sure you have enough space to capture video and photos. If you're using a gimbal, make sure that the batteries are charged and that it is in the desired angle. If you are using a GoPro camera or some other Wi-Fi–enabled camera, make sure that Wi-Fi is turned off so that it doesn't interfere with your drone's navigational controls. Figure 9-3 shows a GoPro camera screen indicating that Wi-Fi is disabled.

Figure 9-3:
Disable
your GoPro
camera's
Wi-Fi before
flying.

Courtesy of Mark LaFay

Flying Your Drone

There are a few last steps you must take before you can take off. These are more universal as they pertain specifically to launching; however, each task may be slightly different from drone to drone. So refer to your user's manual when in doubt. When you're getting ready to launch your drone, your attention must be solely on the task at hand. If you have other distractions, you must put them aside so that you don't injure yourself, and then follow these steps:

1. **Place your drone on the ground in a location that is safe for taking off and for landing.**

   Keep in mind that if your drone has an auto-return mode, it will return to this location on autopilot. Most auto-return modes do not have the capability to avoid collisions. For this reason, you definitely want an open area if you intend to use this feature. Ensure your drone is pointed away from you and that your takeoff and landing pad is at least 10 feet in front of you. Using your own launching pad ensures that you always have a clean and level location for your drone to take off and land.

2. **If your camera is integrated with your drone, make sure that the lens cap is removed, and set your camera to the desired mode for flight.**

   If your camera is an add-on like a GoPro, power on your camera and ensure the cap is removed, and then set your camera to the desired mode for flight.

3. **Verify that your transmitter is off and throttle is set to zero before connecting your drone battery.**

   The chances of your drone firing up when a battery is connected are slim, but you still want to proceed with caution.

4. **Connect the drone battery, and power it on.**

5. **Calibrate your drone.**

   Your drone contains several high-end sensors that need to be calibrated before each flight to ensure that your controls aren't confused. When calibrating, make sure that you are away from any electro-magnetic sources, such as speakers and power lines.

6. **Initiate GPS lock.**

   GPS lock is the same as establishing a home location. Several drones come with an auto-return mode. You will want to reconfigure before every flight if you change takeoff and landing locations. If you do not update your home position, your drone may attempt to return to an old location which could be far away.

   If you plan to fly in heads free mode, when your drone GPS locks, it will orient controls to the current location. You can find more information on flight control modes in Chapter 8.

7. **Arm your drone.**

   Arming your drone means it is ready to fly. This also means do not handle your drone. If you are using any sort of assisted flying mode (meaning you aren't in manual mode), picking up your drone might cause the drone to think that it needs to spin the motors to correct and level out. When your drone is armed, stay at least 10 feet away.

8. **Slowly increase throttle to spin-up your motors and get airborne.**

   After you have taken off, you may want to hover above the ground about 10–20 feet for a minute to verify that your drone is under control. Before heading out, perform one last check of your controls to ensure that you have directional stability as well. Figure 9-4 shows a drone hovering a good distance above the ground for verifying aerial stability.

Figure 9-4:
Use your body as a reference for how high to hover your drone to verify stability.

Flying with an RC

Flying with a remote control (RC) transmitter means that you will be limited to flying line-of-sight, meaning you can't fly what you can't see! Flying with an RC transmitter also means that you won't have the benefit of advanced communication that comes with smart devices like phones and tablets. Figure 9-5 shows a DJI transmitter. The left stick is for throttling up and down, and yaw (left and right turning). The right stick is for moving forward and backward (pitch) and strafing left and right (roll).

Ironically, RC transmitters like the one pictured in Figure 9-5 have the capabilities of controlling a drone for long distances. Probably distances that are outside of your line-of-sight. RC controls do not communicate any position data or battery charge status. For this reason, you need to refer to your manual to determine how you can keep track of battery life with your device.

If you are flying with an RC transmitter, consider having an additional person with you to act as a spotter. Your spotter should stand in an elevated location and should have binoculars to keep a close eye on your drone as you fly it further from your eye's sight.

Figure 9-5:
DJI flight
transmitter
controller.

Source: Tom Reynolds/Creative Commons

The DJI phantom, for example, has an external LED panel that indicates several things using various combinations of colored lights. When the rear LED flight indicator beings to slowly blink red, you must immediately fly the drone back and land it as soon as possible. If you continue to fly despite the low battery, the drone will automatically begin to descend and land in its current location. Figure 9-6 shows the DJI LED flight indicator.

In addition to paying attention to the battery status of your drone, you need to make sure your RC transmitter batteries are fully charged. Losing power to your transmitter will cause you to lose control of your drone immediately.

Calibrating your RC transmitter

With the number of sensors in your drone that must be constantly calibrated, you may not be surprised to hear that your RC transmitter must also be calibrated from time to time. Every drone's transmitter is calibrated differently so you must refer to your drone's documentation for instructions.

Figure 9-6:
The DJI
LED flight
indicator.

Source: WalterPro4755/Creative Commons

As an example, following is the instruction for how to calibrate your transmitter for a DJI Phantom:

1. **Set the S2 switch to the OFF position.**

2. **Set the S1 switch to the GPS position.**

3. **Push the Throttle stick to the top position, and push the Pitch stick to the top position.**

   Keep the Pitch stick at the top position manually since it can return to the central position when released.

4. **Turn the transmitter power switch to the ON position.**

   The transmitter will give a repeating audible response.

5. **Toggle the S2 switch to the CL position.**

   The transmitter gives an audible response, indicating that you are in calibration mode. (During this period, the Throttle stick and the Pitch stick must be kept at the top position at all times.)

6. **Release the stick and Pitch pull the Throttle stick to the central position.**

7. **Toggle the switch S1 to the ATTI position.**

    The transmitter will give a repeating audible response.

8. **Move all of the sticks throughout their complete range several times.**

9. **Put the throttle stick to the bottom position.**

10. **Toggle the S2 switch to the HL position.**

    The transmitter will give an audible response indicating that the calibration has been successfully completed.

Flying with smart devices

Some drones offer advanced flight controller applications that run on a smartphone or tablet. The Parrot AR Drone 2.0 works exclusively with their tablet application. Figure 9-7 is a screenshot of the Parrot AR drone control interface.

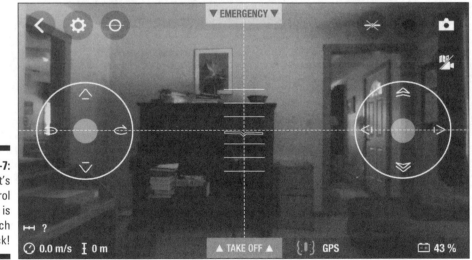

Figure 9-7:
Parrot's control interface is high-tech and slick!

Courtesy of Andrew Amato

The DJI drones can work with an app in conjunction with an RC. The 3D Robotics drones also work with advanced applications as do the Pocket Drones. Flying with a smart device has clear benefits, such as:

✔ **First person flight:** Fly with a video feed from the front of the drone. It's as if you were in the cockpit flying.

✔ **Advanced GPS controls:** Plot a map that contains multiple GPS coordinates, and your drone goes on autopilot and hits each location. This is great if you want to be free to control only the camera. GPS tracking also communicates location back to your control so that you know precisely where your drone is at all times.

✔ **Diagnostic data:** Track what your drone is doing at all times with a visual display. The drone's computer streams battery data to your smart device, giving you a real-time status of the charge remaining in your battery.

RC transmitters do not give you all of the high-end features that a smartphone or tablet controller might. But smartphone and tablet controllers don't have the range that an RC transmitter does.

To use a smart device with your drone, you need to pair the smartphone or tablet with the drone. The application will likely have instructions for how to do this and you can always refer to your device's user manual. If you have a Parrot AR Drone 2.0, use the following directions to connect your phone to your drone:

1. **Start by connecting your AR Drone's battery.**

   The drone's system light will turn green indicating when you are ready to move to the next step

2. **Using your iPhone, tap the settings icon.**

   The settings screen loads, revealing several options for configuring your iPhone.

3. **Locate the Wi-Fi button and tap it.**

   The Wi-Fi settings screen loads, presenting you with the option to connect to any detected wireless networks in the area.

4. **Select ardrone_parrot wireless network.**

   Your iPhone indicates that the connection was successful by placing a checkmark next to the network in the Wi-Fi settings screen, as shown in Figure 9-8.

Landing

Many pilots will tell you that takeoff and landing tend to be where the majority of accidents happen. You can minimize this by ensuring that your takeoff location is clean, dry, level, and stable. However, even with the best launch pad, landing can be tricky because of the turbulence that you may experience during a descent.

Chapter 6 covers an effect called *vortex ring state.* If you descend too quickly, you can get caught in your downwash (air that your propellers are blowing down), and this can cause you to lose control of your drone. To avoid this potential bringer of pain, do not descend faster than indicated in your drone's user manual. As you approach the ground, you will experience a substantial amount of turbulence called *ground effect.* Ground effect occurs when there isn't enough space for air being blown downward through your propellers to dissipate. This causes turbulence and can cause your drone to become unstable. Hovering a few feet above the ground for a few seconds helps reduce this effect. Figure 9-9 is a picture depicting how ground wash occurs.

The best approach for landing your drone is to slowly pull down on the throttle so that your drone descends at a controlled rate. When the drone touches down, simply pull the throttle all the way down and hold it there until your motors shut off. Many drone users who have trouble landing successfully resort to a method called *catch landing.* With one hand the pilot will lower the drone until it can be grabbed with the other hand at which point the motors are killed (see Figure 9-10). The obvious risk here is that the drone will bump into you or your catcher. This is a real risk.

Figure 9-9: Ground wash can cause unmanageable turbulence if you aren't careful.

Source: © Crown copyright 2015/SAC Dave Turnbull/ Creative Commons

Figure 9-10: Catch landing is not for people who are accident-prone.

Source: Sam Beebe/Creative Commons

It only takes one unexpected breeze to send a drone crashing into a person attempting a catch landing. Proceed at your own risk.

Once on the ground, disarm your drone and power it off. For good measure remove the battery as well. Then power down transmitters, cameras, and anything else that is sucking power.

Knowing What to Do in an Emergency

Several variables can affect your flight experience. You might lose control of your drone because you flew out of range, or you may encounter some sort of radio interference that disrupts communication between your transmitter and drone. Unexpected precipitation or inclement weather might make flight dangerous. Battery failure or simply not noticing the charge status of a battery can make a crash imminent. Or maybe you've simply flown your drone far enough away that you can no longer determine its heading and properly pilot it home. Regardless the scenario, if you have control of your drone and things are getting a little dicey, land immediately. Once you've landed your drone, you can retrieve it and start all over. If you lose control of your drone, you could be out of luck unless your drone has a return-home and land failsafe.

Thanks to GPS, drones can establish location data and reference that data throughout flight. Before you start flying, read your user manual to verify whether or not your drone has a fail-safe mechanism in the event communication is lost between the transmitter and drone. In order to take advantage of this feature, you must make sure you establish or update your home location. This location will be where your drone takes off. If you are using your drone for the first time, be sure to engage your GPS lock and then test it during your first flight.

To test your return home failsafe, follow these instructions:

1. **With your Home location established, throttle up your motors and lift off.**

2. **Fly your drone 50 to 100 feet away from you, and then turn off your transmitter.**

   Your drone should automatically return within a few feet of the original takeoff location.

3. **Let the drone finish the exercise before re-launching and commencing with your flight plans.**

One problem with this feature is that most drones lack collision detection. Without a human pilot controlling the drone, it will fly the most direct route back to home, which happens to be a straight line. The drone will collide with anything in its path. To accommodate for this potential problem, you might be able to intercept the drone by re-establishing a connection. Refer to your user's manual to determine the procedure to do this.

There has been a lot of discussion within the industry about how to make drones more self-aware with collision detection capabilities. Five years ago, this may have been categorized as science fiction, but it's coming soon. Maybe as soon as 2015. Several drone startups like DroneDeploy, Airware, and Ascending Technologies are developing drones that use micro cameras that perceive objects and movement. Intel is leading the charge with their Realsense 3D camera.

Chapter 10

Choosing When and Where To Fly

Recreational flying with your new drone should be a lot of fun. Don't get me wrong, it's going to take quite a bit of practice to get used to remote controlled flying, but you will be rewarded with hours, days, even years of enjoyment. Whether you are a seasoned flyer or you are getting ready to take to the skies for the first time, the timing and location for your aerial antics require a little planning. You need to make sure you understand the different environmental variables that can affect your safety, the safety of your drone, and the safety of others. Flying indoors can present risks of damage to people and things. Flying outdoors has its own bag of tricks, as well. Obstacles, wind patterns, precipitation, and temperature, even the amount of light you have, can greatly impact your flying experience.

As you get more confident and experienced with flying your drone and taking advantage of all of the different navigational controls it offers, you will likely become more daring with when and where you decide to fly. Location won't matter nearly as much to you as it will when you first start flying.

In this chapter, you see how to pick a good location for your first several flights. Stay safe and keep your drone airborne by picking a good location and time for earning your wings. Keep reading to learn more about how environmental variables can impact your flying experience. Flying by night and around people also require a stomach for risk and an understanding for how to keep people safe and your drone operational.

Most drones today are designed to fly under a milieu of conditions, but they require experienced pilots to navigate them successfully. Understanding what you are up against in different environments before you take off will set you up for success sooner than later. Then it all comes down to practice.

Choosing a Location for New Pilots

Learning to fly your drone will probably take a bit of time, and you and your drone will probably take some lumps along the way. For your first several flights, you get comfortable with how your drone starts, calibrates, takes off, and lands. You also get accustomed to the controls, flight ranges, auto features, advanced tracking, and even how the device handles with various weather variables. For these reasons, when you first fly, choose an environment that is as forgiving as possible. That means a place where you can recover from a crash with the least amount of damage to you, your drone, and other people's property.

Following is a list of places and things that are *not* ideal for new drone pilots:

✔ **The backyard:** Really, your front yard is not ideal, either. Unless you have a massive chunk of land in the middle of nowhere, learning to fly in your neighborhood is not ideal because of the possibility to hit trees, fences, your house (or your neighbors). Populous neighborhoods mean you also run the risk of crashing into people and their personal property. None of which is good for you or your neighbors. Of course, you can't forget about power lines. Most city neighborhoods do not have the benefit of buried power lines and this can propose a potentially catastrophic situation for you.

Figure 10-1 is a picture of a typical city neighborhood. Most of the houses in the image have next to no yard and are very close together making this area not fit for beginner drone pilots.

Drones are still controversial because of the general public's perception of them as being used to further erode the right to privacy. Many drones are being used with out care or consideration for others. Be thoughtful of your neighbors when flying your drone at or around your home.

✔ **Near any body of water:** If you are flying near or over water, you are testing fate! A stiff gust of wind, bad battery, mishap with the controls, or an auto feature gone wrong could send your drone into the drink and render it useless. Even if the body of water is small, out of the way, and seemingly harmless, it could prove to be a great temptation as you become more comfortable with drone flight. Skimming over the water with a drone is pretty cool. But you might want to save yourself the temptation by avoiding locations with bodies of water.

Courtesy of Mark LaFay

Figure 10-1: Aerial view of a city neighborhood.

✔ **Public parks or other public destination:** Anyplace where you are likely to be around other people that are engaging in activities other than drone flying is not a good idea. Chapter 7 goes into great detail on how to keep you and others safe when you fly your drone. Public areas like parks, sports fields, school yards, and so on are all places where people are engaging in different types of activities and won't be tuned into the aerial acrobatics happening overhead. It only takes one badly tossed Frisbee, strong kickball kick, or Peyton Manning-esque toss of the football to mean disaster for your drone and the people below. Avoid these sorts of public areas. Figure 10-2 shows a great wide open space that is not ideal for flight because of all of the activities happening on the ground.

✔ **Utility easements:** A utility easement is a chunk of land that may be privately owned but has been commandeered by the government for public utilities like electrical lines. An area where there are overhead lines, easement or otherwise, is not a good place to cut your teeth as a pilot. A stiff breeze, slip of the thumb, or maybe an overconfident beginner can spell disaster for your drone or worse. Figure 10-3 is a picture of a utility easement that looks great for flying, but don't be deceived. The lines in the sky can equal sudden doom for a careless pilot.

✔ **Indoors:** It goes without saying that learning to fly your drone indoors is simply not a good idea. Unless your house is massive and has 40-foot vaulted ceilings, or you happen to own your own private gymnasium, flying indoors is, well, actually, it is still a bad idea. When you are learning to fly, you want to leave yourself as much margin for error as possible. Take walls, ceilings, and expensive things (other than your drone) out of the equation so that you can increase the chances of success for your first few flying experiences.

Figure 10-2:
Fun activi-
ties can
equal
disaster.

Figure 10-3:
Utility ease-
ments are
not the best.

✔ **Wooded areas:** You guessed it, like walls, trees are not good for drones. If you're on a camping trip and your campground is nice and open except for the 70-foot hardwood trees everywhere, it's probably not a good idea to fire up your drone for a test flight. No matter how cool the footage might be of your camera bobbing and weaving between deciduous monsters, steer clear of drone-killing trees.

Now that you know where and what you should avoid for those first few flights, it probably sounds like you need to be in the middle of the nowhere. That's not the case; you simply need to be mindful of things that can destroy your drone, or harm you or others and their property.

A location that is wide open, free of obstructions, and is not populous is ideal for beginning pilots. An added bonus would be if your location had soft ground. Soccer, baseball, or football fields are all great places (assuming they aren't occupied). Flying at times when people aren't likely to be around is also a good consideration. Parking lots after hours are a great option as well. Just watch out for the landings!

Tall grass can complicate finding a downed drone, but it can provide an equipment-saving crash medium.

If you opt to fly in a public place that is likely to be used by other people for other activities, consider planning your fly times at off-peak times. Also consider bringing in orange cones or flags, as shown in Figure 10-4, to denote the

Figure 10-4: Cones and flags are great for making others aware of your drone flying antics.

area where you intend to fly your drone. You can't block people from entering your temporary fly zone, but you can use the cones or flags to notify folks of the activity within the cone zone.

Flying Indoors

Flying indoors presents a unique set of risks and challenges, such as flying into people, furniture, ceilings, and floors. If you have pets, you have to be concerned with their curiosity with the flying chew toy. All of that aside, in case you want to fly inside, the following sections offer some tips to set you up for success.

Securing the area

Before you fire up your drone and take to the indoor "skies", run through the following checklist to ensure a safe, and successful flight:

- **Make sure pets are out of the area.** If you are flying at home, make sure that your pets are secured so that there is no possibility of them coming into the room while you are airborne. If you are flying in a public place, post notices and markers indicating the area of your flight.

- **Move or remove furniture from the room.** In the event that your drone uses sonar to maintain altitude, this will save you the headaches of unexpected jumps and drops. If you need furniture in the room for a video that you are capturing with your drone, then consider rearranging the furniture so that your drone's flightpath is free of objects that may interfere with your flight.

- **Reset your drone.** Don't forget that modern drones are advanced machines with advanced computers. Your drone will remember flight conditions, settings, and other variables that, if left unchecked, could make flying your drone increasingly more difficult. Resetting your drone will erase its memory and set you up for a fresh start. Most drones will come with a reset button. However, you may want to refer to your manual to ensure that you are resetting the device appropriately.

- **Adjust your flight controls.** Many drones will allow you to have multiple control settings so that you can set different sensitivity levels for your flight controller. Make sure that your drone is either set to a pre-set for indoor flying, or manually reduce your drone's control sensitivity. The last thing you want is to tap a directional control and have your drone go flying into something. Configuring controls is specific to the drone so be sure to refer to your drone's user manual to learn how to adjust the sensitivity of your flight controller.

Knowing your drone

Every drone functions a little bit differently. For example, some drones use pressure gauges to determine altitude. Other drones use sonar to determine distance from the ground. Knowing how your drone functions helps you avoid disaster. For example, if your drone uses sonar to calculate altitude, when you fly over a structure like a coffee table, your drone may quickly adjust thinking that all of a sudden it lost 2 to 3 feet of altitude. Soft materials absorb more sonar than they reflect, so if your drone goes over a couch, it may autocorrect thinking it is higher than it should be. Knowing these nuances could save you from calamity.

Using an indoor hull

Some drones come with a hull that shields the propellers from impact. If your drone supports an indoor hull or some sort of propeller guard, use it. If you get too close to a wall or a person the hull or shield will reduce the likelihood of a drone, or human, casualty. Figure 10-5 is a picture of a Parrot drone with a protective hull attached and also without.

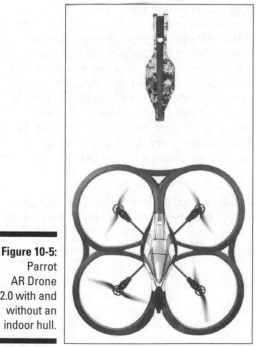

Figure 10-5: Parrot AR Drone 2.0 with and without an indoor hull.

Courtesy of Tucker Krajewski

Avoiding ceilings, floors, and walls

It may seem obvious, but it can't be stated enough. For drones to get airborne they must move a ton of air. The propellers force air down, which causes the air pressure below the drone to be higher than average and the air pressure above the drone to be lower than average. This creates a force called *lift*, which takes the drone airborne.

When you fly very close to the ground, the air is forced more sideways than down, which causes the drone to become unstable. If you fly too close to the ceiling, air can't flow downward to the propellers and instead comes in from the sides. The air pressure then decreases even more, creating a vacuum effect and thus drawing the drone closer to the ceiling. Avoiding walls is smart, as well, because the flow of air is impeded as you get closer to a wall, affecting the lift. Your drone will tilt toward the wall causing it to fly toward the wall and imminent doom. The rule of thumb is to fly in large, uncluttered rooms with high ceilings.

Stocking up on spare parts

This goes for flying in general but definitely if you are planning to do indoor flying. The odds are in favor of you crashing your drone, and it is a rarity to have a crash and not break something on your drone. Flying with damaged parts is not ideal because it can throw off your drone's stabilization, causing it to fly erratically. For example, a damaged propeller, even if it is the most minute of defects, can cause your drone to be unbalanced. Propellers are highly refined pieces of aerodynamic equipment. Slight variances in weight can make them move differently. Cuts or breaks can cause air to move over the propeller differently. Both of which will cause your drone to not function as it would with un-damaged propellers. That's not safe for you or for your drone. In addition to spare parts, have a first aid kit on hand just in case the hard object your drone crashes into is you, your pet, or someone else.

The most cost effective way to stock up on spare parts is to go to sites like www.amazon.com, robotshop.com or even on ebay.com. You can always go to your drone's manufacturer's website to shop for parts. This is covered in greater detail in chapter 11.

Flying in Sub-Optimal Weather Conditions

The best weather for drone flying is when it is sunny, a reasonable temperature (75 degrees Fahrenheit, for example), and little to no wind. The reasons for this are simple: sunny days are beautiful, 75 degrees is simply the perfect temperature, and flying in the wind is a pain in the rear. Besides being a more enjoyable experience, there is some science to flying in mild temps. Flying in wind can be difficult and will drain your drone battery faster than normal. Cold temps cause batteries to lose charge faster. Rain is detrimental to anything electronic and high heat isn't because drones produce quite a bit of heat on their own. Extreme heat can put unnecessary wear and tear on batteries and computers. But the reality is that you will probably want to fly in weather conditions that don't always fit this profile. Flying on cloudy days or days that are hot or cool aren't so much a problem. It's the days that are freezing, precipitating, or extremely windy that are particularly troublesome.

Rain and snow

Flying in precipitation is a surefire way to ruin your drone for good. It goes without saying that water and electronics don't mix. Most drones are not waterproof, or water resistant. Think of your drone as being the Wicked Witch of the West. A little bit of water is going to bring your drone to a dramatic end. A good policy to have is that if it is raining, even just misting, you should keep the drone bundled up inside and away from its arch nemesis.

Flying a drone in snow is not as bad of an idea as flying in rain, but it can still result in damage to your drone. Flying in snow is great because it makes for great pictures and video. However, flying in snow is difficult for some drones that utilize cameras for stability and navigation. This is because the white snow provides little to no contrast for the cameras to discern movement.

WARNING!

Whether the snow is falling from the sky and onto a drone that's airborne, or if your drone crash lands into a pile of the white fluffy stuff, snow is not friendly to drones.

Having reduced control of your drone in a snowy landscape could equal disaster for your drone. Snow is nothing more than frozen water, albeit pretty frozen water, and when snow hits warm batteries and motors, it melts and now you're looking at potentially saturating your electronics and killing your drone.

If you crash your drone in the snow, remove the battery immediately and use a towel to wipe it off. Snow that makes its way into your drone can be blown out with compressed air. The key is to make sure there is no power connected to your drone if it has been exposed to water.

Windy days

Usually with precipitation comes wind, but not always. If you live in Chicago, wind is a normal occurrence and more often than not it isn't accompanied by rain, sleet, or snow. You can fly a drone in wind but if it gets much stronger than 20 mph, you drone will be cruising for a bruising. Flying in wind requires a lot of practice, patience, and back up batteries. Your drone will blaze through batteries trying to maintain any sort of position on a windy day. If you plan to fly on a windy day, watch the batteries and the buildings.

Freezing temperatures

A lesser known environmental hazard is freezing temperatures. This seems counterintuitive because the battery and moving parts on a drone can get quite warm when in use. But the reality is that Lithium Polymer batteries, which are the common battery of choice in drones, drain substantially faster in freezing cold weather. A beautifully sunny winter day with no wind can be a wolf in sheep's clothing so be sure to closely monitor your battery life when flying on a cold day.

Night Flying

Flying at night is a lot of fun and quite a bit more challenging for the obvious reason that it's hard, if not impossible, to see your drone at night. Flying at night is a great way to force yourself to learn how to fly in ways other than by sight. You may also want to fly at night because you want to capture nighttime video footage or photos of landscapes or even nocturnal wildlife in their natural habitat. Of course, you could always fly at night with the assistance of artificial lighting to illuminate your environment, but what's the fun in that?

Before you take to the moonlit skies, consider the tips in the following sections.

Knowing your drone

Some drones, like the Parrot AR Drone 2.0, use external cameras (usually low-quality) to calculate movement and maintain stability. Flying at night with little or no light renders these cameras useless which makes it difficult for the drone to be able to make calculations needed to fly in some necessary flight modes. If your drone is configured in this manner, refer to your manual to determine a way to temporarily disable these cameras. This simple adjustment may disable advanced flight controls, but at the same time, it will free your drone to be flown manually at all hours of the day.

If your drone's orientation cameras can't be shut off, or if you aren't comfortable shutting them off, you can always attempt to attach downward facing lights on the bottom of your drone. Figure 10-6 shows a drone equipped with lights for night flying! Lighting the ground makes it possible for your drone's cameras to see and therefore function as intended. Your drone's altitude will, however, be limited by the strength of your lighting. The higher you go, the less focused the light will appear on the ground below, which will make the cameras less and less accurate.

Figure 10-6:
Night flying
is possible
with down-
ward lights.

Creative Commons Credit: Goldmann Jo, U.S. Fish and Wildlife Service/ Creative Commons

Downward facing cameras are generally used to calculate movement and distance from the ground. This is particularly useful when flying in an auto-pilot mode for maintaining a specific altitude. Not many drones use this technology and newer drones have implemented sonar for detecting distance from the ground.

Understanding advanced piloting controls

Flying during the day gives you, the pilot, the option to fly by sight. In fact, at the time this book was written, the standing FAA policy for hobby drone flight is that you cannot operate a drone out of your line of sight. However if you intend to fly at night, unless the area where you are flying is well-lit by parking lights or some other form of artificial light, you will need to get comfortable with flying by GPS or first person video. For first person video to be useful, you will need to make sure there is some sort of light on the front of drone that would function similarly to how headlights on a car work.

Attaching lights to your drone

Flying at night makes it nearly impossible to fly your drone by sight, unless you attach lights to your drone so that it can be spotted at great distances. Personally, I think this is a great solution because it makes your drone look like a UFO. If your drone does not come with, or support, a night-lighting kit, try wrapping your drone with thin strips of LED lights.

Flying at night without any sort of GPS locator or independently powered lights can be risky in the event you have a crash. A night of flying can quickly be turned into a frustrating night of searching the countryside for your downed drone. Make sure you know the area where you are flying and always give your drone your undivided attention.

Flying in Populated Areas

Flying outside in sparsely populated rural areas is great because you do not have to worry about accidents that could harm other people or their property. You, like many people, may live in an urban area where great open spaces aren't very close by, however. That means you will either need to find the great wide open spaces of the rural world, in your urban setting, or learn how to cope with your surroundings.

Here are some tips for flying in an urban area:

- ✔ **Always be aware of your surroundings.** In cities, you have to worry about people, pets, buildings, and property that does not belong to you. Try to avoid flying over houses, cars, and other expensive items that do not belong to you. Definitely do not fly over people if at all possible and never for a second should you take your eye off your drone while you are midair.

- ✔ **When you are taking off and landing, always announce your activity.** This way, people in the area know what is going on. Loudly state something like "Drone take off" or "Landing my drone!"

- ✔ **If your drone comes with the option for protective hulls or propeller guards, use them.**

- ✔ **If you haven't bought a drone yet and you are trying to pick one out, purchase a lightweight drone.** The lower the weight, the better it is for the person underneath it if it fails and falls to the earth.

- ✔ **Respect your neighbors and other people in the area.** If you are flying in a public space and someone expresses their discomfort for the activity, land immediately and go somewhere else. There is no sense stirring things up.

- ✔ **Don't break the law.** Chapter 7 discusses the current laws and how to stay up on changes in the law. While you may be able to get away with flying above 400 feet in the air out in the country, if you break the law in the city and someone gets hurt as a result, the ramifications could be substantially greater.

Drones are a subject of major controversy right now, and while it is perfectly legal to fly a drone for fun, there are numerous people that are uncomfortable with them. Flying in an urban area exposes you to greater scrutiny, so be sensitive so that your actions don't negatively affect the drone community.

Many people are dubious about drones. When flying your drone, you should be courteous, thoughtful, and inviting to those around you. If you are met with resistance, then consider going elsewhere with your drone. The drone community at large will benefit from your empathy for those around you.

Chapter 11

Maintaining Your Drone

• •

In This Chapter

▶ Performing routine maintenance

▶ Creating a post-flight checklist

▶ Storing your drone

▶ Repairing your drone

▶ Finding parts and support online

• •

Drones require great care. Chapters 9 and 10 show you how to fly a drone starting with pre-flight checklists. When you finish flying, you don't want to just toss your drone in the garage until you are ready for your next flight. There is an extensive amount of work that should be done prior to packing away your drone. In this chapter, you review a sample post-flight checklist and get tips for creating your own. Your post-flight checklist will walk you through inspecting your device for damage, cleaning up your drone, inspecting and handling batteries, and storing your drone.

As you continue to log hours flying your drone, your chances for crashes or hard impacts will increase. Drones are durable but not indestructible, which means that in time you will need to repair your drone and replace parts. By the end of this chapter, you will know how to shop for parts online, find technical support so you can do your own repairs, and in the event your repairs are extensive, you will know how to find a repair technician. This chapter is all about how to take care of your drone so that it lasts.

Post Flight Maintenance

Drones are complex pieces of machine and computer technology that require great care to ensure their longevity. If taking time to clean up and care for things is not in your DNA, then you may be in for a surprise when you get up and running with your drone. After every flight, you must inspect all parts of the drone for damage and integrity. Even if you successfully fly your drone without making hard landings, colliding with objects, or crashing, normal wear and tear can build up over time and cause problems in future flights.

Here are some issues that can arise during flight:

- ✔ Flying in wet conditions can cause rust.
- ✔ Flying in dry conditions can cause dust buildup.
- ✔ Drone motors produce a great deal of vibration, which can slowly loosen tight bonds and bolts or screws.
- ✔ Bugs can chip, ding, or otherwise gunk up your propellers.
- ✔ Impacts and crash landing can damage propellers, propeller guards, landing gear, hulls, batteries, camera gear, and more.

Creating a post-flight checklist

In Chapter 9, you see how to create a pre-flight checklist. In this chapter, you see how to create a post-flight checklist. If you use a post-flight checklist, you don't have to leave anything up to memory. Every drone is different, so there is not a standard post-flight checklist that applies to every drone, but the core of the post-flight checklist is similar across the board. To get you started, the following sections cover some examples of what might appear on a post-flight checklist along with some explanations of what you are looking for and why it matters, and a picture to help you better visualize how a post-flight check list is configured.

Having a post-flight checklist will be critical to ensuring the success of your drone flying experiences. Your post-flight check list and your pre-flight check should ensure that you are never flying with dirty cameras and damaged equipment. Spend some time getting to know your drone and customize the checklist covered in the following sections to be a better fit for your equipment.

❏ Power off your drone

Before you inspect and dismantle your drone, make sure it is disarmed and that your batteries, drone, flight controller, and any other powered equipment are turned off.

If your drone is not disarmed, the propellers may turn on to stabilize the drone if it is picked up or moved, which can result in serious injury. Always ensure that your drone is disarmed before you handle it. Figure 11-1 shows the arming status indicator on a Pocket Drone.

Figure 11-1: Verify that your drone is disarmed by checking its status indicator.

❏ *Inspect the body of the drone*

Look over your entire drone to check dirt, dust, water, grime, bugs, or any other sort of filth buildup. Cleaning the drone makes it easier to find any damage that may have been otherwise hidden. Once the drone is clean, look over its body to check for cracks or breaks. Figure 11-2 is a picture of the body of a Pocket Drone that has been cleaned.

❏ *Inspect the propellers*

The propellers are the blades that spin at a high rate of speed to move air and create lift, which causes your drone to be airborne. Propellers are carefully balanced to ensure that at high speeds, they do not create any unnecessary vibration that could make your drone difficult or unfit to fly. Chips, cracks, or any sort of damage no matter how big or small will result in your propeller needing to be replaced. Crashing your drone into an object will almost always ruin unprotected propellers. Flying through bugs can do the same! Figure 11-3 is a picture of the propellers of a Pocket Drone. Notice that one has been chipped.

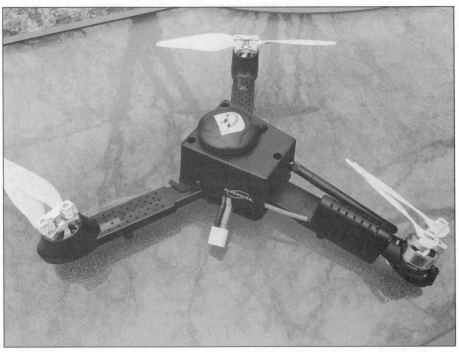

Figure 11-2:
The body of
a very clean
Pocket
Drone.

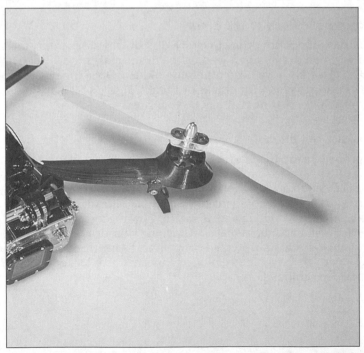

Figure 11-3:
Damaged
propellers
must always
be replaced.

❏ *Propeller guards and protective hulls*

Some drones come with the option to add a protective shield around the propellers. The Parrot AR Drone 2.0 has a very light protective hull that goes around the entire drone. The point of these is to protect the propellers and the body of the drone in the event of an impact. These protective shields, however, can be damaged as well. If your protective hull is damaged, it can cause your drone to become unbalanced and unstable. Also, if a damaged protective hull is involved in another collision, the hull could flex or broken pieces could go into the propellers causing a crash and substantial damage. If your protective hull is broken, replace it. Figure 11-4 is a picture of an intact protective hull on a Parrot AR Drone 2.0.

❏ *Batteries*

Drones require heavy duty, Lithium Polymer batteries (LiPo) because of the amount of power they require to stay airborne. The problem with LiPo batteries is that they are far more dangerous than the batteries you typically find at home. LiPo batteries are extremely volatile and must be cared for. If your battery is damaged, you must dispose of it. Damaged batteries can cause fires or even explosions. Figure 11-5 is a picture of a LiPo battery that has been damaged.

Figure 11-4:
Parrot
AR.Drone
2.0 protec-
tive hull.

Source: Yutaka Tsutano/Creative Commons

Source: Carlos Sancho/Creative Commons

Figure 11-5:
Damaged
LiPo
batteries are
hazardous
to your
health.

If your batteries made it through your flying unscathed, then disconnect them and let them cool down before charging them.

For more information regarding the safe handling and use of LiPo batteries, see Chapter 6.

❏ Fittings

Drone motors produce a substantial amount of vibration and if any parts of the motor are loose, the vibration can dramatically increase. Loose fittings can cause parts like propellers, motors, and other attachments to shake, rattle, and roll, causing your drone to become unstable. Ensure that your fittings are snug so that nothing comes loose during your next flight. If your previous flight seemed rougher than usual, check the fittings. Figure 11-6 shows the propeller fitting of a Pocket Drone.

❏ Landing gear

Landing gear can be fixed or retractable. Retractable landing gear has many more parts that must be inspected to ensure that the gear continues to retract and extend as designed. You also must inspect landing gear to make sure that there are no cracks or breaks. Hard landings can have the same effect on your landing gear as a crash landing. Figure 11-7 shows the landing gear on a Pocket Drone.

❏ Wiring

Your drone has numerous wires that send power throughout the device. The main wires you will come in contact with are attached to a harness that quickly connects your battery to your drone. When you check your drone after a flight, check the wiring harness to ensure that there are no loose connections. It is also good to check all visible wires for cracks, breaks, burns, or any other sort of damage. There is a lot of juice flowing through your drone and any sort of wiring issue could cause your drone to fall from the sky. Figure 11-8 is a picture of the wiring harness on a Pocket Drone.

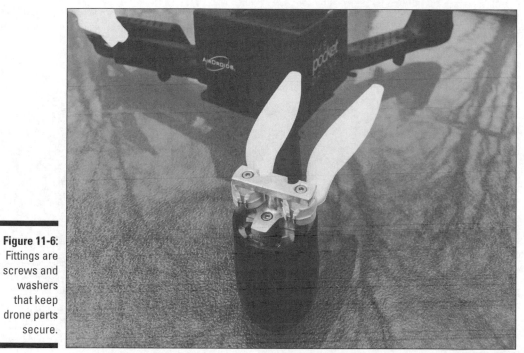

Courtesy of TJ Johnson

Figure 11-6:
Fittings are
screws and
washers
that keep
drone parts
secure.

Figure 11-7:
Pocket
Drone
landing
gear,
cute and
effective.

Courtesy of TJ Johnson

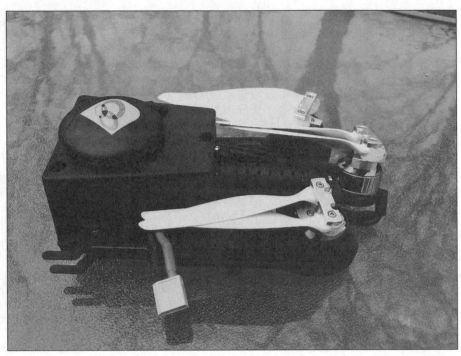

Figure 11-8:
Pocket
Drone
wiring
harness.

❏ *Download flight info*

Some drones will track and store flight information so that you can review it after you are done flying. Some of the information that is tracked includes speed, altitude, and GPS location. The more you fly, the more information your drone will take in until your storage is completely filled. Some drones store flight information on a removable storage device so that you can download, review, and archive it. Be sure to download this information and archive it, or at least clear it off so that you have space to record flight info, when you need it.

❏ *Download camera data*

If you are flying and taking pictures and video, you always want to be sure to dump your footage onto a storage device and clean the image and video data off your drone's camera. If your drone uses removable media to store video and photo data, be sure that you put the storage media back into your drone when you have cleaned off the data. Nothing is worse than getting out to a location and finding that you left your storage media at home or have no room on your device to take new pictures and video. Figure 11-9 shows the Parrot AR Drone 2.0 USB flight recorder.

Figure 11-9:
The Parrot
AR Drone
flight
recorder.

❏ *Clean camera and lens*

Several years ago I was tasked with recording video footage of life on the road with a rock and roll band called Haste The Day (www.hastetheday.us). I was good with a video camera but I wasn't disciplined enough to have any sort of checklist to review before shooting. After a several months of filming I noticed that my lens was dirty and the filth showed up on a decent chunk of footage that I captured in Africa. Five years later I look at that footage and kick myself for not checking the lens to ensure it was clean. Don't be that guy! If cleaning your lens is on your preflight checklist (covered in Chapter 9) and your post-flight checklist, you don't have to worry about lens spots on your camera.

Storing your drone

You must ensure that you have a safe place to store your drone. If you did not get a storage case with your drone, then it is well worth it to invest in one.

Following is a list of things you should consider when shopping for a storage case for your drone:

✔ **Excess storage:** Keeping all your drone gear in one place is the best way to ensure that you have what you need when you go flying. Choose a case that is a snug fit for your drone and offers storage compartments for a battery charger, extra batteries, extra parts, flight controller, and any other critical equipment.

✔ **Waterproof or resistant:** To some, this may be overkill, but a waterproof case never hurt anyone (unless it fell on your head). Waterproof or water resistant cases are great if you plan to take your drone to places where it will be exposed to wet conditions.

✔ **Hard or soft shell:** If you're planning to take your drone on long trips where you may want to check it on a plane or put it in a trailer, a hard shell case is the way to go. Hard shell cases such as those made by Pelican can be waterproof and almost bomb-proof.

Regardless of what you decide to store your drone in, you must take great care in how you store your drone's batteries. LiPo batteries require great care. LiPo batteries have a storage capacity that can be diminished if they are not stored properly.

Here is how to properly care for your LiPo batteries to ensure a safe and long life:

✔ **Half-charge:** LiPo batteries should not be stored fully charged. Doing so will slowly erode the battery's storage capacity, shortening its useful life. Most battery chargers come with a *storage mode* that will charge the battery to 40%-50% which is an adequate charge level for storage.

✔ **Keep cool:** LiPo batteries produce heat when they are used. The heat then causes the chemical reaction to produce more heat which can speed the power drain process. By reducing the battery's temperature during storage, you reduce the rate at which they will lose charge and overtime this will preserve their storage capacity.

Store your batteries in the refrigerator to ensure they last as long as possible. Only do this with half-charged batteries; never place fully charged batteries in the fridge. Also, never leave your batteries in a hot place, such as in your car in the summer.

✔ **Moisture control:** If you store your batteries in the refrigerator, you must let them warm to room temperature before you plug them in to charge. During this time, your batteries may experience a buildup of condensation. Storing your batteries in plastic bags will protect them from atmospheric moisture as they are warming to room temperature. Figure 11-10 is a picture of LiPo batteries being stored in plastic bags in the refrigerator.

Courtesy of Andrew Amato

Figure 11-10:
Safely
storing LiPo
batteries
in a
refrigerator.

DIY Repairs and Maintenance

If your drone needs a tune-up, don't worry. You don't have to send it in to have a repair technician work on it. You can make the repairs on your own. Several resources are available online where you can find the answers you need to repair your drone. Before you scour random message boards, however, visit the website of your drone manufacturer. For example, if you purchased a Parrot AR.Drone 2.0, follow these steps to get help online:

1. **Using your computer or web-enabled device, launch a web browser and go to www.parrot.com.**

   The Parrot website appears.

2. **Click the support link located at the top of the web page.**

   The support homepage appears.

3. **Locate your drone model on the screen, and click its associated link or icon. If you are looking for support for the AR Drone 2.0, click its icon located in the center of the screen.**

The Parrot AR Drone 2.0 support site appears. On this site you will find several videos and documents that will help you navigate common repairs. Figure 11-11 is a screen shot of the Parrot AR Drone 2.0 support website.

4. **If the videos and information contained on the support site do not help you repair your drone, contact the support staff using the email or phone number located at the top of the screen.**

Larger and more prominent drone manufacturers are more apt to have a robust online database of help documents, videos, tutorials, and other useful information for repairing your drone. This is one major benefit to buying a drone from a major manufacturer like DJI or Parrot. That is not to say that the milieu of startup drone companies should be avoided. These companies are creating quality products that, in many cases, can take non-manufacturer specific replacement parts.

If you are having a hard time finding information for fixing a particular issue with your drone, you should look into the various drone support groups and online communities. Chapter 4 goes into how to find and navigate these forums in great detail.

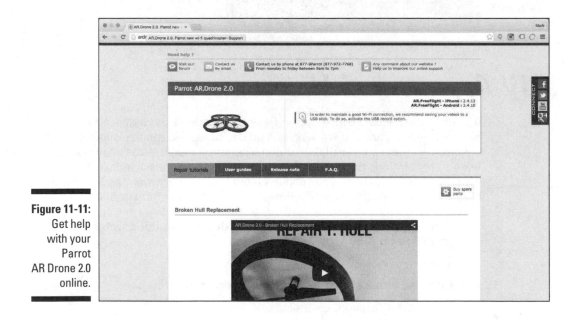

Figure 11-11: Get help with your Parrot AR Drone 2.0 online.

How to find replacement parts for your drone

Purchasing spare parts for your drone is a good idea whether you need them or not. The part you will replace most often is your propellers, simply because they are the most likely to get trashed if you run into objects or crash land. It is always good to have a couple spare sets of propellers on hand so that you can repair your drone and get back up and running in no time. You can find replacement parts by going to your device manufacturer's website. For example, if you own a DJI Phantom 2 drone, purchase replacement parts, like propellers, online through DJI by following these steps:

1. **Using your computer or web-enabled device, open a web browser and go to** `www.dji.com`.

   The DJI website will load.

2. **Locate the Store link at the top of the screen, and move your mouse cursor over it.**

   A submenu appears revealing several options.

3. **Locate and click on the** `Tuned Propulsion Systems` **link.**

   A page filled with various propeller options appears as shown in Figure 11-12.

Figure 11-12: Shop for replacement Phantom drone propellers at dji.com.

4. **Locate the set of propellers you want, and click on the item.**

   The product page appears, giving you all pertinent information on the propellers.

5. **If you would like to purchase the propellers, click the Add To Cart button to add them to your cart, and follow the on-screen directions to complete your purchase.**

Sometimes purchasing parts from your device manufacturer is not the most cost-effective option. You can also look for replacement parts on Amazon and eBay.

Finding a drone technician

If you aren't confident or prepared to repair your drone yourself, it may be time to hire a drone technician. If you purchased your drone from a major manufacturer such as Parrot or DJI, first determine whether your repairs can be covered under your device's warranty. To do this, you need to refer to the instruction manual that came with your device. If you find that the repairs are not covered under the warranty, you need to pay for the parts and labor.

Make sure you don't void your manufacturer's warranty by doing something inadvertently. To make sure you're always in compliance, check the manufacturer's website. It is generally a good idea to not dismantle your drone, fly it in the rain or crash into water, modify your drone with unapproved parts, or lose your proof of purchase.

Parrot Drones does not offer repair service for anyone living outside of the UK. So if you own a Parrot drone, you need to contact the retailer where you purchased the drone to get service for your device. If you purchased a DJI drone, you can send your drone back to DJI for repairs. To do this, you must first contact the DJI service and support team in your region. To get these contacts, visit them online at www.dji.com/service/repair-service.

Sending your drone into a technician can take quite a bit of time, depending on the number of drones that are already waiting to get service. This can mean extended amounts of downtime before you fly again. Before you commit to sending in your drone, see if you can get the help you need online to perform the repairs on your own or go to your drone manufacturer's website to see if they have a listing of authorized repair centers or a listing of retail partners. You can contact these locations to see if they will repair your drone in shorter time.

Part IV
Aerial Photos and Videos

In This Part . . .

- ✔ Shooting photos and video
- ✔ Dealing with shaky footage
- ✔ Working with aerial photos and images

Chapter 12

Capturing Beautiful Photos and Video

*T*aking great photos and videos is a precise blend of science and art. Excellent photographers first must have a vision for the image they wish to capture. Then they must understand how their equipment works so that they can be sure to dial-in the settings to capture that image.

Taking a photo or video with a camera in your hands is vastly different than taking a photo or video remotely from a moving vehicle like a drone. You will have fewer controls and remember, aerial photography is action! That means you will have little to no time to adjust on the fly. For this reason, automatic settings will quickly become your best friend. You can prep on the front end for light, however.

By the end of this chapter, you will understand the fundamentals of lighting in photography and you will have enough information to get you ready to capture great photos and video from your drone, regardless of time and location.

The Importance of Light

Light is the single most important component for photography. In fact, without light, you can't capture photographs. To photograph something, you must have a light source to illuminate the subject of your photograph.

Light is a general term used to describe the visible portion of the electromagnetic spectrum. Visible light is comprised of colors ranging from red to violet. Infrared and ultra violet are both in the visible spectrum but require special equipment for human eyes to see.

You can use several types of light sources. In a natural setting, you work largely with the sun. If you shoot at night and rely on natural light, you work with sunlight reflecting off the moon (and maybe some starlight). You may also work with light emitted from a fire, whether it be logs burning or a candle.

To capture images indoors, you work with some sort of artificial light, such as lightbulbs or light produced by combustibles such as a kerosene lantern, candles, or fire in the fireplace. Lightbulbs come in many shapes and sizes. Incandescent bulbs are the oldest form of lightbulb. Fluorescent tubes and compact fluorescent bulbs are other types of lightbulbs, as are LED (light emitting diode), Halogen, and Xeon.

Light, whether it is produced naturally or artificially, radiates outward to illuminate an environment. When light hits an object, some colors are absorbed, and some are reflected back. Your eye sees what is reflected back and that, in a very rudimentary sense, is how you are able to see objects.

Cameras work similarly to how your eye works. When you open the camera's lens shutter, light is allowed in for a brief moment. In digital cameras, the light is focused onto a sensor that functions much like your eye. The image information is turned into 1s and 0s and saved as a file. In film cameras, the light is focused onto a reactive material called *film*.

You might think that if little-to-no light is bad for capturing photos, a ton of light is the way to go. Not so fast! This isn't the case. If you have ever stood outside on a particularly sunny day, the light is almost so bright that it hurts your eyes and requires you to put on sunglasses. Plenty of light is good for capturing pictures, but too much light can cause just as many problems for your camera as it does for your eyes. Thankfully, your action camera, point-and-shoot, and even your DSLR all come with auto features that will address the issue of too much and too little light so that you can focus on other things.

Light Direction

Quantity of light is extremely important when planning your shots with your aerial camera. Light levels aren't the only thing you need to worry about when considering the lighting of your shot. You need to also be concerned with the source and direction of your light. Light radiates outward in all directions from its light source. If the subject of your photo or video can see the light source, then it is in direct light, which means that it will receive the maximum amount of illumination that the light source provides. Direct light is important for emphasizing the difference between light and dark.

The direction in which your light shines on your object, whether it be natural light or artificial light, is also very important. There are four basic types of directional lighting:

✔ **Soft light:** If you have ever been outside on an overcast day, you might have noticed that while you couldn't see the sun, the world was still illuminated. Direct light tends to cast several shadows and the brightness can cause nuances of color to be lost while soft light allows those colors to be seen. Naturally colorful objects are best shown in soft light, as opposed to direct light. Figure 12-1 shows a setting with soft light.

Figure 12-1:
Overcast days provide great soft light.

Courtesy of Tucker Krajewski

✔ **Front light:** When the light source is to the back of the camera or photographer, it is shining on the front of the subject of the photo or video. Front light is fantastic for illuminating the front side of your subject and casting shadows behind it (or him or her). This can create depth in your image by separating the subject from the background. When front lighting, the angle of the light source can greatly impact the photo. As the light source moves higher above the subject, shadows will shorten and the image will appear more flat. Figure 12-2 shows a setting that is front-lit.

Figure 12-2:
Front light
a subject to
pop colors
and create
depth.

✓ **Side light:** When your light source is illuminating your subject from the left or right, you will see much more texture in the subject. This is because one side of the subject will be illuminated causing the other side to have shadows. The side light creates contrast and is great for dramatic photos. Side light can occur naturally when the sun is very low in the horizon and the camera is at a 90 degree angle to the horizon. You can also create side light with artificial light by placing a light source to your left or right. Figure 12-3 shows a setting that is side-lit.

✓ **Backlight:** When the light source is located directly behind the subject of your photo, the camera will be pointing in the direction of the light source. Backlighting creates shadows on the front side of your image. If your subject has a unique shape, the lighting will bring that to life by shining through the edges. Backlighting can be tricky to work with. Figure 12-4 shows a setting that is backlit.

It will be rather difficult to control the light source when you are capturing aerial photos and video with your drone. However, understanding how the angle and position of light can impact your images will help you make decisions on where and when you fly your drone.

Figure 12-3:
Side lighting
can create
dramatic
color and
black-
and-white
photos.

Courtesy of Tucker Krajewski

Figure 12-4:
Backlighting
creates dra-
matic and
beautiful
images.

Courtesy of Tucker Krajewski

White Balancing Like A Pro!

You've likely noticed that light bulb technology has been changing over the last 10 years. Instead of just incandescent bulbs, there are compact fluorescent lights (CFL) and LED lights as well. These new light bulbs can produce as much light, or more, as incandescent lights but with lower amounts of energy required. The change in technology has brought to light, pun intended, the fact that not all light sources produce the same color of light. When planning a video or photo shoot, the different concentrations of color can impact your photos and video drastically! The human eye and brain have an uncanny ability to detect and adjust what we see based on the light source. Cameras, however, are not as clever! That means they need a little help. Most cameras come with a feature called *white balance*. This feature is used to give your camera a frame of reference for what white looks like with the current light source.

Flame, incandescent bulbs, fluorescent tubes, compact fluorescent, and the various types of natural light all produce different concentrations of reds, blues, and greens. This variation in color is called color temperature and is measured in Kelvin (K). The next time you purchase a lightbulb, spend some time looking at the packaging to see how it describes the light it emits. Figure 12-5 is a scale that describes the color of light produced by various light sources. Light sources with lower Kelvin ratings tend to produce more reds than light sources with higher Kelvin ratings, which produce more blues.

Most modern digital cameras will come with multiple white balance settings. This is so you can adapt to the various environments and light sources to produce the highest quality visuals as possible. Most devices come with an auto white balance feature, but unlike the human eye and brain, digital cameras are not great at auto adjusting white balance. Figure 12-6 shows common white balance settings found on modern photo and video cameras today. Take the time to get to know your camera's settings and practice with different white balance settings so that you can capture the best images possible. You may want to rely on the auto settings for ease of use; however, getting familiar with the different auto settings will give you a better picture of what to expect.

Working in Low Light

Light is the critical component to capturing great photos and video; however, in some cases light is in short supply. Unfortunately, if you don't have a camera that is designed to work well in low light, you may be out of luck.

Temperature	Source
1,700 K	Match flame, low pressure sodium lamps (LPS/SOX)
1,850 K	Candle flame, sunset/sunrise
2,700–3,300 K	Incandescent lamps
3,000 K	Soft (or Warm) White compact fluorescent lamps
3,200 K	Studio lamps, photofloods, etc.
3,350 K	Studio "CP" light
4,100–4,150 K	Moonlight[2]
5,000 K	Horizon daylight
5,000 K	Tubular fluorescent lamps or cool white/daylight compact fluorescent lamps (CFL)
5,500–6,000 K	Vertical daylight, electronic flash
6,200 K	Xenon short-arc lamp[3]
6,500 K	Daylight, overcast
6,500–10,500 K	LCD or CRT screen
15,000–27,000 K	Clear blue poleward sky
These temperatures are merely characteristic; considerable variation may be present.	

Figure 12-5: Different light sources have different color temperatures.

Source: PAR/Creative Commons

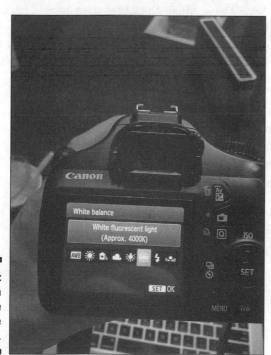

Figure 12-6: Camera white balance settings.

Courtesy of Mark LaFay

Digital cameras capture images and video by focusing light onto a sensor which then translates the image information into a digital file. Naturally, the bigger the sensor, the more light information it can capture and store. Which means that cameras with bigger sensors tend to work better in low-light conditions than cameras with smaller sensors.

Action cameras and point-and-shoot cameras are compact cameras with small sensors which means that by nature, they don't perform the best in low-light scenarios. However new advances in camera technologies have provided incremental low-light performance increases. If you are planning to work in a low-light environment with your point-and-shoot camera or action camera, check your camera to see if there is a low-light feature.

If you are using a GoPro, the GoPro Hero4 Black has a low-light feature that can be engaged with the GoPro mobile application for your iPhone or Android.

If your aerial camera is a DSLR camera with interchangeable lenses, you can set it to work in low-light by adjusting the following items:

✔ Use a lens with a larger aperture. Aperture is usually denoted on a lens with an "F" number. The smaller the number, the larger the amount of light that is let in.

✔ Crank up the ISO on your camera. ISO simply has to do with how sensitive the sensor is to the light. In older film cameras, ISO was the speed of the film. The higher the number, the faster the speed. This is good for low light as well as action photography.

✔ Lower your shutter speed so that light has more time to enter. With aerial photography on a drone, long shutter speeds can mean blurry footage so be cautious of how slow you set your shutter.

✔ For still cameras, shoot to RAW photo files because RAW has no compression meaning all of the information captured by the camera is saved. This allows you to extract more image details later. These files are usually pretty large in size so you may want to make sure you have extra storage on hand.

✔ For video, reduce the frame rate to 24 frames per second.

Working with low-light will require a bit of trial and error until you are satisfied with the quality of imagery that you are able to capture with your equipment.

Choosing a Video Resolution

Video has evolved quite a bit in the past few years. It seems like only yesterday when the world was enamored with 400 pound tube televisions with flat, no-glare screens. Now it's all about super mega ultra-high definition (not the technical term), lightweight and thin LCD or LED televisions. Suffice it to say, television technology has leapt forward in a short period of time. For the most part, the primary advertising point is screen resolution. Resolution largely means the number of pixels that can fit on your screen and it is measured in terms of vertical and horizontal rows of these pixels.

For example: High Definition televisions have 1920 horizontal rows of pixels and 1080 vertical columns of pixels. Just as standard definition has gone the way of the dodo, High Definition will soon follow suit thus making the way for higher definition televisions like 2k (2048x1080) and 4k (3840x2160). Figure 12-7 compares high definition, 2k, and 4k resolutions.

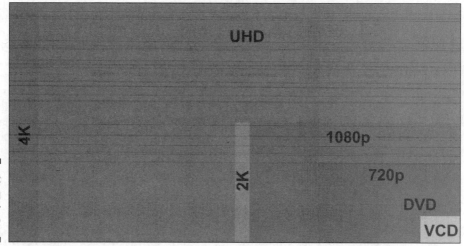

Figure 12-7: How big is your resolution?

Source: Jamvanderloeff/ Creative Commons

Before you start capturing aerial video with your drone, you will want to give some consideration to what resolution you want your video to be. Below are some considerations you should give before deciding on your video resolution:

✔ Most televisions today are high-definition, so shooting in a resolution less than HD may not look all that great on your television.

✔ Ultra High Definition will capture much more picture information and will look great on an ultra-high-definition television.

✔ The higher the resolution, the more the camera will have to work which means the shorter the battery life. How long do you intend to film?

✔ Ultra-high definition televisions are not readily available yet which means that your Ultra-high-definition video footage may have to be scaled down to accommodate today's TVs losing some of the advantage you may have from shooting in ultra-high-definition.

✔ Processing Ultra High Definition video footage requires pretty substantial computer equipment. If you shoot in Ultra HD, you may not be able to do anything with it other than stream it from your camera to your TV.

Choosing a Frame Rate

At a very rudimentary level, video is nothing more than a sequence of pictures captured at a high rate of speed. The frame rate of your video is the number of pictures that are captured per second and this number is referred to as frames per second (FPS). Common frame rates for video capture and playback include 24.7FPS, 30FPS, and 60FPS. High-definition video is commonly shot at 30 or 60FPS. Regardless of which frame rate you choose to shoot at, you must play your video back at the same frame rate. Otherwise your video will play back at a different time.

For example, if you capture aerial footage at 60FPS, and you decide to play the video footage back at 30FPS, one second of video recorded will equate to 2 seconds of video played back. That means that your video will play at half the speed at which it was recorded. This is great if you like to watch videos in slow motion!

Speaking of slow motion, if you actually want to capture action shots and play them back in slow motion, you will need to opt for an extremely high frame rate. The newest GoPro action camera will capture HD footage at 120FPS. If you capture footage at 120FPS and then slow it to 30FPS for playback, it will take 4 seconds of play time to watch 1 second of recording. That means your footage will play back at 25% the speed in which it was shot! The really high-end slow-motion cameras will capture footage at frame rates in excess of 1000FPS. Figure 12-8 is a sequence of frames shot at 30FPS on the top and a sequence of frames shot at 120FPS on the bottom. If you aren't intending to capture video footage for slow-motion playback, choose a frame rate at 60FPS or less. Generally, using 30 frames per second reduces the size of the files and makes the videos easier to work with.

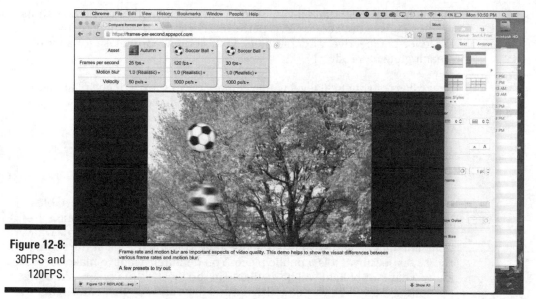

Courtesy of Mark LaFay

Figure 12-8:
30FPS and
120FPS.

Planning Your Shoot

If you are planning to use your aerial camera rig purely for fun free of any need or expectation to capture high-quality photos or video, you can skip this section. If you are interested in capturing fantastic photos, however, you will need to understand how to plan your shot before you shoot it. Shot plans can be extremely complex depending on the level of production you are planning to put on. For instance, if you are using your drone to capture footage for a commercial or a video, then you might have quite a few different components such as models, actors, and choreographed movements. Regardless of the complexity, your shot plan should consist of the components described in the following sections.

Purpose

Understanding why you are shooting and whom you are shooting for should be the first step in shoot planning. If you are using the footage for an advertisement or some sort of marketing piece, identify the shots or images that will help you communicate your message. Knowing the audience will also drive the images and how those images might be caught. If you are capturing some concert footage, are the images and video for you or for someone else? How will the content be used and who is the intended audience? This may help you understand if you need to have wider and more distant shots vs. close ups; more audience vs. performer; or more band perspective vs. audience perspective. Understanding your audience will make for a more meaningful end product!

Regardless of your skill level with a camera or your experience planning, directing, and shooting pictures and video, trial and error is a great way to learn. Remember Hollywood wasn't built in a day!

Location

Have a plan for where you intend to shoot. There are numerous variables that come into play when deciding where to shoot. If you are shooting indoors, you will *definitely* want to know the room dimensions, know what objects might be in the way, and understand traffic patterns in the room or rooms, especially if it is a public place. You definitely want to make sure you know what sort of light will be available in the location. If you are shooting outdoors, you will be working with natural light and supplemental lighting may be necessary depending on the day and timing. If you are shooting indoors you will want to know what type of lighting you are working with and if there is a blend of lighting due to large windows and such.

If you are shooting outdoors, you will definitely want to see the location to get a feel for whether or not there are other people to be concerned with. What sort of overhead objects need to be accounted for, such as power lines, street lights, and trees. Lastly, you will want to make sure that you have backup locations in mind in the event something unforeseen happens. Also, when selecting a location, make sure you keep the purpose of your shoot in mind as it may drive location-specific decisions like angles, directions of moving footage, etc.

Timing

The time of your shoot is going to be more critical when shooting outdoors than it is indoors. The reason is that outdoor shooting can be a breeze when you have full sun and great whether to help you along. However, if you are planning for more dramatic shots like dawn or dusk shots where you have long shadows and lower light, you will have less time to work with. Light, as you know, is a critical component to shooting photos and videos and the sun works on its own schedule so planning is critical.

Execution

Once you have a grasp on the purpose of your shot and the intended audience, and you have the location locked in and your schedule locked down, you are ready to execute your shoot. The next thing you do is plan for what you are going to shoot and how you are going to shoot it. You might consider calling this your shot plan. Much of this is subjective and may require trial and error, but you should still think through the point of the video shoot, and the story you mean to tell.

Then you need to plan the different ways you want to capture it. For example, if you are doing an aerial shot of a building, you may want to plan to shoot from the ground up because it makes the viewer feel like they are being elevated and uplifted. The opposite, shooting from the top to the ground might communicate landing, safety, and stability. The overall scope of your shoot needs to drive the execution portion of your shot plan.

Planning is the key to a successful shoot. Anticipate as many variables as possible, know your audience, and aim to connect with them. Most importantly, you should have fun. Flying + filming = fun.

Chapter 13

Working with Shaky Footage

One of the hardest parts about watching home videos, aside from reliving childhood memories that are neatly tucked away into the nether regions of your long-term memory, is sitting through the motion-sickness inducing camera work. Maybe you dislike other aspects of home videos, but I've always been the first to get nauseated by fast, jerky camera movements. Chances are good that your family didn't intend to make movies that looked liked they were shot during the "big one" in southern California. It was probably a combination of a lack of technology, know-how, and experience.

When shooting with a drone, you don't have the benefit of stable ground to keep your video footage from shaking. Drones are flying aircraft that have nothing but aerodynamics to rely on for aerial stability. A soft breeze can make your footage feel like it was shot on the open seas during a hurricane. Even on the stillest of days, the vibration from your drone's motors can create enough motion to make your video blurry or, in some cases, unwatchable.

Several tools are available that you can use to improve the quality of your footage by reducing the amount of shake that is picked up by your aerial camera rig. In this chapter, you see different camera techniques that will enhance your footage by reducing shake. You also see how to use some advanced flying techniques to smooth your video.

Using Camera Tricks to Minimize Shake

Have you ever noticed when taking photographs that sometimes your images are blurry or out of focus? Your images may be blurry for several reasons. It could be that your camera wasn't in focus, or it could be that the subject was moving or you weren't able to keep the camera completely still while you were capturing the photo. Walking, laughing, sneezing, or an unsteady hand can make video footage look like it was shot on the open sea during a hurricane.

If you want to remove blur from photos or shake from videos, you can get a fixture like a tripod or stand or, if you're a low-tech shooter like me, you may just want to stack some books on a table to give you the steady aim that you need. When you take photos with your drone, however, you don't have the luxury of a tripod or a sturdy shelf to stabilize your camera. In fact, you have even more variables working against you.

Following is a list of several factors that could impact the quality, and stability, of your aerial photos and videos:

- ✔ **Lighting:** Chapter 12 covers the importance of light in detail. If you work with less than ideal lighting, your camera has to do more to compensate for the lack of light needed to capture a quality image. When you have adequate light, your camera has more options to help you capture the desired image.

- ✔ **Weather:** Rain, snow, and most important, wind greatly impact the clarity of your photos and stability of your video. Precipitation can make moving parts work less smoothly and wind, depending on how strong it is, will take your drone to task.

  Your drone is not employed by the postal service and therefore is not meant to be used in rain, sleet, or snow (or gloom of night, but that's beside the point). Avoid flying your drone when conditions are wet.

- ✔ **Pilot experience:** Newer pilots may not have the skill to use the controls well enough to fly straight and steady. Skill with the controls means a more stable flight and better video.

- ✔ **Mechanical issues:** Chapter 5 covers the various parts of your drone. A finely tuned flying machine ensures that you have a minimal amount of shake and vibration.

- ✔ **Camera quality:** It goes without saying that the better the camera, the better the chances you'll have stable video and clear photos. Image stabilization, shutter speeds, sensor sizes, and so on impact the quality of the video.

Camera adjustments to sharpen photos

Blur in photos is often caused by movement. The movement of your subject may cause the blur, or the movement of the camera may cause it. The obvious answer is to stop moving; however, that's not easy when you take photos with a drone. You have numerous variables that make it next to impossible to have a completely steady shot. Depending on your camera, there may be hope.

If your drone comes with an integrated camera, read the user manual about the camera's features. Chances are good that your drone manufacturer added features designed to help you capture crisp photos. Keep in mind, however, that drone manufacturers focus on building great flying machines, not cameras. This means your integrated camera may only do a great job when there is plenty of light and a skilled pilot at the controls.

Most add-on cameras come with auto features designed for *action photography,* or shooting moving subject matter. If you made the decision to purchase an action camera, then your camera is designed almost exclusively for the purpose of capturing moving images or images while you are moving. Using auto settings on your camera isn't "cheating." Rely on auto features as much as you can because this will give you more mental bandwidth to focus on great flying and enjoying the experience of capturing aerial photos. If you don't have auto settings or you are unsatisfied with your auto settings, you need to adjust your camera settings manually to compensate for your environment.

Following is a list of settings you will need to tweak to get great results:

- ✔ **Shutter speed:** Reducing the effects of motion on your photos means that you need to shorten the amount of time that your shutter is open. In situations when there is a lot of light, this won't be a problem. Shooting in low light, however, may prove to be somewhat difficult because a fast shutter speed may not allow enough light in to capture an image.

- ✔ **ISO:** In traditional film cameras, the rate at which your film could absorb light was referred to as *film speed.* In digital cameras, the rate at which your camera's sensor absorbs light is your ISO. Action photography typically requires an ISO of 800 or higher. However, the lower the light, the higher the ISO must be.

- ✔ **Lens:** If you are working with a camera that supports interchangeable lenses, you will want to opt for a lens that offers image stabilization and has a low F-stop number. As the F number gets smaller, the amount of light that comes in gets larger.

Advanced flight modes

The more flight conditions you fly in, the more comfortable you will become and the steadier your flights will be. Smooth flight is important when capturing smooth video and sharp photos. Even the most skilled drone pilots, however, may find that advanced autopilot modes are the best way to capture superb photos and video.

Each drone manufacturer offers a different bag of tricks with their drones and drone flight controllers. As discussed in Chapter 2, you should consider the autopilot modes that your drone offers when purchasing your drone. They could make your life much easier.

Autopilot modes can be a great way to stabilize your flight, especially if you are a less experienced drone pilot. Autopilot does not, however, replace the intuition and creativity of the human pilot. In time, your flight skills will continue to improve and while autopilot technology will get more advanced, it will be a long time before they can ever truly replace a skilled human operator.

Follow-me mode

The Pocket Drone, shown in Figure 13-1, comes with an autopilot feature that enables the drone to follow you using GPS tracking in your Android tablet controller. The Pocket Drone is designed to follow behind at a pre-set distance, by using your android tablet as a tracking beacon of sorts. This feature is exceptional for capturing footage of a specific subject as it moves.

Figure 13-1:
The Pocket Drone offers a follow-me mode.

Courtesy of TJ Johnson

The Pocket Drone doesn't offer collision detection. For this reason you must be sure to use follow-me mode in an environment free of objects that could cause a collision.

Director mode

The Parrot AR Drone 2.0, shown in Figure 13-2, offers a Director mode, which gives you several options for controls specifically designed to capture video footage. This includes a modes to simulate up and down movements of a crane, panorama rotations, and Travel mode to simulate dolly movements.

Programmed Flight mode

The DJI Phantom drones, shown in Figure 13-3, give you the option to program a flightpath using GPS coordinates (some models require an upgrade module to enable this feature). Once the course has been charted, you can set the drone loose and then focus your energies controlling the camera, but be prepared to take control of the drone If something goes awry. You will need to ensure that your flightpath is at an altitude that will avoid any potential ground clutter, but other than that, this is a great feature if you can plan your shots accordingly.

Figure 13-2:
The Parrot
AR Drone
2.0.

Source: Lima Pix/Creative Commons

Source: B Ystebo/Creative Commons

Figure 13-3:
DJI
Phantom
drones offer
several
high-end
autopilot
modes.

Altitude Hold mode

Several drones, including the DJI Phantom drones, allow you to set an altitude for your drone and leave it to maintain the altitude until otherwise indicated. This features is excellent for gathering stationary shots at an absolute height above the ground.

Stabilizing With a Gimbal

A *gimbal* is a support system that allows an object to remain horizontal regardless of the motion around it. Gimbals were widely used in waterborne vessels to keep instruments, equipment, and even drink holders upright with respect to the horizon regardless of the motion of the boat. Drone gimbals keep a camera in the same position regardless of the motion of the drone. Figure 13-4 shows a diagram of how a very basic gimbal works.

Similar to how you would use gimbal technology to ensure that you don't spill your cup of coffee on the rough seas, a gimbal can keep your aerial camera in a specific position regardless of the movement of the drone around it. To fully understand how a gimbal works, you must first under-stand the three axes of aerial movement specific to an airplane. Refer to Chapter 8 to learn about the different movements along the X, Y, and Z axes known as pitch, yaw, and roll. A gimbal is designed to keep your camera at the same angle regardless of the movement of the drone by automatically compensating using calibrated and often remotely controlled electric motors.

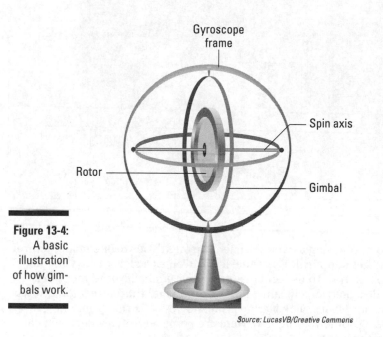

Figure 13-4:
A basic illustration of how gim-bals work.

Source: LucasVB/Creative Commons

How to find a gimbal for your drone

They sound extremely high-tech but the good news is that you don't need to know how a gimbal works in order to use it. But before you start shop-ping for a gimbal, you do need to know if your drone supports a gimbal. Most of the big manufacturers, such as DJI and Parrot, either have integrated gimbals or an exclusive line of gimbals that you can buy direct or through authorized retailers. Figure 13-5 is a picture of a gimbal being used on a DJI Phantom drone.

Source: B Ystebo/Creative Commons

Figure 13-5:
A drone
gimbal in
action!

The benefit to purchasing a camera gimbal through your drone manufacturer is that you will get support for your device as well as a slew of easy to find documentation on how to use and maintain your gimbal. Not to mention, the gimbal is designed specifically for your drone and therefore should work without any major issues. One glaring issue, however, is that your choices can end up being somewhat limited. Here are some websites where you can find alternative options:

- ✔ **Helipal.com:** This is a one-stop shop for all things drone-related. Search for camera gimbals and in the product descriptions you will typically find comments on what drones the gimbal will mount to. Helipal is great for shoppers outside of the U.S.

- ✔ **ReadymadeRC.com:** This is a great family-owned business based out of Ohio. If you can't find what you need on ReadymadeRC.com, you may be out of luck. Their exhaustive list of products makes it a great option for U.S. and Canadian customers.

- ✔ **Photography Store:** Online photo supply stores, such as B&H or Adorama, are great outlets for finding a broad selection of camera accessories and equipment. If you have another camera website you typically frequent, search for "drone camera gimbal" on the sight, and see what you come up with.

✔ **Amazon.com:** You can find almost anything on Amazon. Search for camera gimbals available through several different companies. This is a great way to price shop, read customer reviews, and even find some support documentation all before you buy.

Choosing the right gimbal

As you continue to research the right gimbal for your drone, you will find that not unlike shopping for the right drone, gimbals also come in many shapes, sizes, and combinations of features. Gimbals designed for specific drones will offer high end features that you may not be able to find from gimbals that are a little more universal. Major features include:

✔ **Number of axes:** Gimbals for drones are either 2-axis or 3-axis. 2-axis gimbals do not compensate for yaw, which means that there will be slightly more bump in your images. 3-axis compensates for yaw, but this feature comes at a cost (naturally). If you are spending the money on a gimbal, you should go for the 3-axis.

Gimbals with three axes are generally heavier than their 2-axis counterparts. A heavier gimbal means shorter flight times. Be sure to prepare to cut your flight shorter than normal when using a heavier 3-axis gimbal.

✔ **Remote control:** One of the benefits to buying a gimbal built specifically for your drone is integration into the flight controller. For example, some gimbals built for the DJI Phantom 2 can patch into the drone so that the camera's tilt angle can be adjusted remotely.

✔ **Camera support:** Gimbals are designed with specific cameras in mind. There are some gimbals that come with support for multiple compact camera types. Primarily, you will find that gimbals are designed with support for the GoPro camera because of its wide use in action sports and aerial photography and videography. Make sure the gimbal you select supports your camera.

✔ **Pre-Calibration:** Calibrating a gimbal can be somewhat tedious for beginners. A gimbal that comes pre-calibrated and ready to simply plug and play is the fastest and easiest way to get up and running. Gimbals made specifically for your drone should almost always come pre-calibrated. Calibrating isn't difficult, but it is one more step you have to take before getting airborne.

Once you have chosen the gimbal for you, installation should be a cinch. Zenmuse is a popular line of Gimbals by DJI that offer supreme technology and ease of use all bundled into one. Before you rip open the package, your best place to start is with the instruction manual or user guide. You can also find several assembly and installation instructions on YouTube. Regardless of what you decide to go with, remember that using any gimbal is better than not using a gimbal at all. The gimbal helps reduce vibration generated by your drone's motors. The gimbal will also stabilize your video and pictures while in flight. If you aren't convinced yet, spend some time on YouTube searching for drone videos shot with gimbals. That will make a believer out of you!

Stabilizing Footage after It Is Shot

Reducing unwanted shaking and motion from your video requires a lot of preparation before you start shooting and as much, if not more, care during your shoot. Camera skills, flight experience, add-on hardware like gimbals, and advanced image stabilization software found in many cameras today can all help you capture the best footage possible. Sometimes, however, no matter how much work you put into it, footage can still come out a bit rough. If you find that your footage is still a little more shaken than stirred for your liking, there is still hope.

Turbo Video Stabilizer

Turbo Video Stabilizer is an affordable action video editing software created by a company called Muvee. This software is less than $20 and boasts some of the best video stabilization available at consumer prices. Their technique is designed to simulate the stability of a gimbal, applying the effect to footage you've already shot. Figure 13-6 shows the Turbo Video Stabilizer website.

Adobe After Effects (AE)

Adobe After Effects (AE) is a high-end video editing software package that offers many tools for the video editing professional. AE can be used for animation, motion graphics, and other advanced video editing. It can also be used for simple yet critical tasks like removing the Harlem-shake from your video. Warp Stabilizer VFX is a plugin for AE that meticulously cleans up and stabilizes video footage.

Adobe After Effects is part of the Adobe Creative Suite that is available to use for a low monthly fee. If you are a student at a high school or university, speak to your advisor about whether or not your school has a negotiated educational discount.

Figure 13-6:
Stabilize
your foot-
age with
Turbo Video
Stabilizer.

Courtesy of Tucker Krajewski

YouTube

Google's video channel is the second largest internet search engine in the world (the first is Google). Recent statistics show that over 100 hours of video footage are uploaded to YouTube ever minute. That's a lot of video footage! As YouTube has grown and evolved, it has begun expanding video editing features on its website. A recently added feature is one that reduces shake from your video. This was initially intended to help clean up video captured with mobile phones, but it is proving to be useful in cleaning up footage captured with aerial cameras, too. YouTube is available almost everywhere around the world, it is free and so incredibly easy to use that it only makes sense to try it out. To remove shake using YouTube's video editor, follow these steps:

1. **Using your computer, you will need to open a web browser and go to www.youtube.com and log into your account. If you do not have a YouTube account, you can register for one at no cost at www.youtube. com.**

2. **Once logged in, click the Upload button located in the top right corner of your web browser.**

The video upload page loads in your web browser, giving you the option to browse your computer for the video you want to upload and edit. Or you can drag-and-drop the video onto this screen.

3. **Drag the video you want to upload and drop it into the browser window where indicated, as shown in Figure 13-7.**

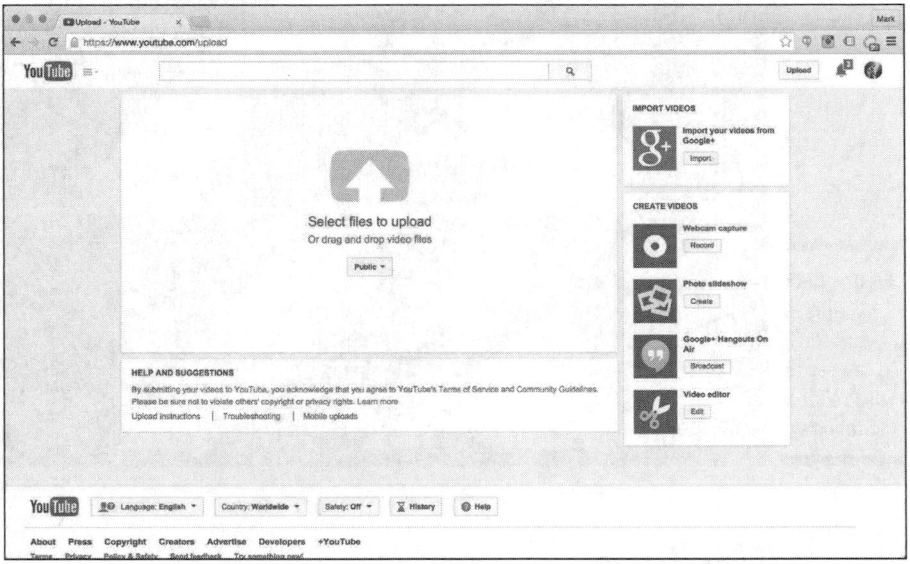

Figure 13-7:
The YouTube video uploader is drag and drop.

YouTube receives the file and uploads it into your YouTube account. You will automatically be taken to the video editing page where you can edit your video before saving and publishing.

4. **Now that your video is finished uploading, click Save Changes to save the video and then click Video Manager located at the bottom of the screen.**

Your browser automatically takes you to the video manager.

5. **Your newly uploaded video will appear at the top of the list; click edit to edit your video.**

Your browser automatically takes you to the video editor where you can edit and manipulate your video.

6. **Once in the Video editor, click the `enhancements` link at the top of the screen.**

The browser window switches to the enhancements screen where you can perform numerous tweaks to your video.

7. **Locate and click the Stabilize button.**

   YouTube processes your video, detecting and removing unnecessary motion from your video. You can preview the changes in the video viewer located in the middle of the screen before saving the modifications.

8. **When you are satisfied with the changes to your video, click Save to save your edited video.**

Chapter 14

Working with Aerial Images and Footage

Capturing photos and videos with your drone takes a lot of up front work. You probably didn't go to the great lengths of buying a drone and learning how to fly it to capture images and video only to never view them or share them with others, right? That's what I thought! Your aerial images may be for use in a movie, work documentation, art, or maybe just for documenting memories. Regardless of why you are using your drone to capture all of this information, you need to know how to get your videos and pictures off your drone and edited, shared, catalogued, viewed, or otherwise used!

The task of moving files off your drone and onto a computer is called importing. Regardless of how your drone or camera is configured, this process can be achieved without too much effort. In this chapter you will learn how to access the video and images on your drone and import them to your PC, Mac, or Chromebook. It doesn't stop there; once images and video are on your computer, you have a handful of options for how to use them.

In this chapter you will review a sampling of photo and video software products that will give you the tools to enhance your images and video, make home movies, and even export your home movies to physical media like DVDs and Blu-Ray©. You will also learn how to share images and video with family, friends, and coworkers using popular internet tools like Dropbox and Google Drive.

Lastly, you will learn how to view your pictures and video on your computer as well as how to stream video and photos to your television from your computer. You can also skip a step and view your photos and video on your television directly from your drone or drone's camera.

Importing Images and Video

Taking videos and photos off your drone's camera or your add-on camera and putting them on your computer is a process referred to as *importing*. Depending on your drone, this process can be done in a number of ways. With some drones, you can actually stream your video or images back to a device while you are flying (the Parrot Drone offers this sort of capability). Other devices have built-in media that cannot be removed, requiring you to plug your drone directly into your computer. The majority of drones and cameras, however, use some sort of removable storage so that your videos and images can be quickly moved to computer and deleted to free up space on the device. This process is called *dumping*.

If you are using a drone with an integrated camera, refer to your device manual to verify whether your drone uses removable media or you have to plug it into your computer directly. If your drone uses an add-on camera such as a point-and-shoot, action camera, or DSLR, chances are that the camera has removable storage. If you are unsure, refer to your device manual to verify.

Cameras typically come with a data port that allows you to plug your camera directly into your computer using a USB cable. Due to the compact nature of cameras, the USB port on your camera will be smaller than the USB port on your computer. The smaller USB port is referred to as a mini-USB. It doesn't stop there. There is an even smaller version of the mini-USB, called micro-USB, which is also commonly used with compact cameras.

The cable that is needed to connect popular cameras such as the GoPro or pretty much every point-and-shoot and DSLR camera on the market is a mini- or micro-USB to USB cable like the cables pictured in Figure 14-1. These cables are typically shipped with the camera or drone (if the drone supports it). If your drone doesn't come with these cables, you can purchase them online at Amazon.com.

To connect your camera to your computer, follow these steps:

Figure 14-1:
The mini- and micro-USB to USB cable.

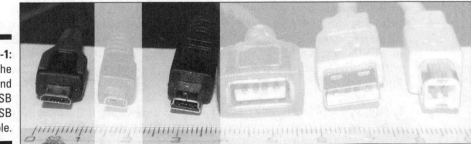

Source: Viljo Viitanen/Creative Commons

1. **Ensure your camera is powered off.**

   Some cameras can be a little temperamental. Ensuring your camera is off before plugging it into your computer will help you avoid any mishaps.

2. **Locate the USB plug on your camera and plug the USB cable into the camera first.**

   USB ports on cameras are typically hidden under a cover of sorts to prevent dust, lint, and other foreign materials from entering the USB port(s). Figure 14-2 is a picture of the GoPro USB & HDMI ports and protective cover.

3. **With the camera still powered off, plug it into your computer's available USB port.**

   Your computer will likely not detect the camera's presence because it is powered off.

4. **With your camera connected to your computer, power the camera on.**

   Once powered on, your camera might indicate that it is connected to your computer. Your computer should also indicate that a camera or removable storage has been connected. This can happen in a number of ways, depending on the type of computer you have and the software that is installed on it. Some computers might open a window containing image and video files. Default photo/video software may load, or a simple icon may appear on your desktop representing your camera's media contents, as shown in Figure 14-3.

Figure 14-2:
GoPro USB and HDMI ports.

Figure 14-3:
MacBook
Pro desktop
with a cam-
era storage
icon.

If your computer has an SD card slot and your camera has a removable SD card, you can also import photos and video from your camera by removing the SD storage card and inserting it into your computer directly.

Once you have verified your camera has been successfully connected to your computer, you are ready to take the next step in moving your images and video from your camera to your computer. There is a good possibility that your computer will load default software for importing, organizing, editing, or otherwise managing photos and video. Some of these popular software tools are covered later in this chapter.

Importing images and video to a Windows machine

With your camera connected to your Windows 8.1 computer and powered on, follow these steps to import images and video to your computer:

1. **From the Windows desktop, right-click and, from the popup menu that appears, choose New.**

2. **Select the option to create a new folder.**

   A folder appears on the desktop. If you don't name your folder now, you can do so later by right-clicking the folder and selecting the option to rename it.

3. **Click the Start button located in the bottom left corner of your screen.**

   The Start menu appears, revealing several options.

4. **Click File Explorer.**

   A window appears, revealing all media currently available for browsing. Windows treats your external camera like storage device.

5. **Double-click the icon for your camera to begin navigating through the contents of your aerial camera.**

6. **Using your touchpad or mouse, click the file or folder you want to import to your PC. If you would like to import more than one file, press and hold Shift, and then, using your touchpad or mouse, click the files and folders you want to import.**

   The files will become highlighted indicating their selection.

7. **Click your selection and drag it to the new folder you created on your desktop.**

   The files will move with your pointer indicating they are being dragged.

8. **Once your pointer is hovering over your destination folder, release your click to drop all of the selected images and videos in their new location on your computer.**

   The files will be copied to the new location on your computer.

Importing images and video to a Mac

With your camera connected to your Mac and powered on, follow these steps to import images and video:

1. **Press and hold Control and then click your Mac's desktop.**

   A dropdown menu appears.

2. **Choose New Folder.**

   A new folder appears with the name highlighted indicating you can type to rename the folder.

3. **Type the new folder name, and press Return.**

   The folder name becomes permanent.

   You can always rename the folder by right clicking on the folder icon and selecting *rename*.

4. **Locate your camera's icon on your desktop, and double-click it.**

   A window appears, revealing the contents of the camera.

5. **Using your touchpad or mouse, click the file or folder you want to import to your Mac.**

   If you would like to import more than one file, press and hold Shift, and then, using your touch pad or mouse, click the files and folders you want to import.

   The files become highlighted, indicating that they are selected.

6. **Using your touchpad or mouse, click your selection and drag it to the new folder you created on your desktop.**

   The files move with your pointer, indicating they are being dragged.

7. **Once your pointer is hovering over your destination folder, release your click to drop all of the selected images and videos in their new location on your computer.**

   The files will be copied to the new location on your computer.

Importing images and video to a Chromebook

With your camera connected to your Chromebook and powered on, follow these steps to import images and video to your computer:

1. **Locate the app menu button in the bottom left corner of your shelf, and click it.**

   The app menu appears, revealing several application options.

2. **Locate the Files application icon and click it.**

   The Files application will load.

3. **Your camera appears in the list of media options on the left side of the Files window.**

   Click on the camera in Files to begin browsing its contents.

4. **Holding Shift, click the files you want to import to your Chromebook.**

   The files become highlighted indicating your selection.

5. **When you finish selecting files, click and drag your selection to the folder that you have designated as the home for your images and videos.**

   The files are placed in the folder.

If you need a little extra help with your Chromebook, check out my book: *Chromebook For Dummies* (Wiley), to get a little helping hand!

SD Cards and SD Card Readers

Many of the drones and add-on cameras available today record images and video to a removable storage device called an *SD card*. *SD* stands for secure digital and was introduced to the world in 1999. This storage format is fantastic for portable electronics such as phones and cameras because it is compact, non-volatile (meaning it doesn't require electricity to remember its contents), and high-speed, and now SD cards are available in larger capacities.

SD cards have become the unofficial standard for compact photo and video devices. In fact, the SD association touts that SD cards are used in over 8,000 different devices across 400 brands around the world. That's a lot of love for SD! The greatest benefit to the drone community is that SD cards are lightweight and easy to swap out. They are also durable and affordable, and as technology continues to grow and expand, SD cards are continuing to shrink. Currently, SD cards come in a standard size as well as mini and micro.

Most drones and action cameras utilize the microSD storage cards while many point and shoot cameras use miniSD cards and standard SD cards. DSLRs are increasingly using standards SD cards almost exclusively.

You can import your images and video from an SD card by inserting your SD card into an SD card slot on your computer, or by using an SD card reader. Most computers accept only standard SD cards, so if you are using a micro or miniSD card, you will need to plug it into a standard SD card adapter. If your computer isn't equipped with an SD card slot, you must use an SD card reader. SD Card readers are small devices that connect to a computer using a USB cable. SD card readers will give you the option to import from any size SD card which alleviates the need for an SD card converter. Figure 14-4 is a picture of a USB SD card reader that accepts all sizes of SD cards.

Importing images and video from an SD card is the same as importing images and video directly from a camera. Start by inserting your SD card into your computer directly or with an SD card reader. Once connected, simply follow the steps outlined in the previous sections.

Digital file storage has come a long way in the last 10 years. SD cards are much more stable than their predecessors. However, SD cards are not immune to failure. Make sure you take care of your SD cards by storing them in cases and try to not touch the metal contact points that are plugged into cameras and computers. When possible, back up the contents of your SD cards even if they aren't full. That way you are protected in the event of a catastrophic failure of your SD card!

Source: King of Hearts/ Creative Commons

Figure 14-4:
One-size-fits-all SD card reader.

Viewing Images and Video

The greatest hurdle for digital photo and video technology has been processing real-life images, which have an infinite amount of information, into a digital format, which has a finite amount of information. To do this, image processors take the information and begin stripping out bits that may not be detectible by the human eye. This process is called *compression*. There are a lot of ways to compress photos and videos and the net result is several different types of photo and video file formats. These different file formats require different software to be able to process files using those formats and display their information back to you in the form of a beautiful photo or video on your computer screen.

For the most part, drones and the majority of cameras you might use with your drone save images and video in file formats that don't require special software to access. That is, your computer's operating system should be able to open them without any additional software.

Following is a list of widely supported image and video file types:

- ✔ **Common image file types:** JPG/JPEG, TIF/TIFF, PNG, BMP, GIF
- ✔ **Common video file types:** MPG/MPEG, MP4, MOV, WMV, 3GP, AVI

If your drone's integrated camera or your add-on camera output to different file formats, you may need to use additional software to be able to view or edit the files. Software is covered later in this chapter.

If your camera produces files in one of the listed formats, you should have no major problem viewing the file on your computer. Simply locate the file and double-click it. Your computer launches an image previewer or video player, depending on the file you selected.

Picture Editing Software

A major advantage to digital photography is that you can do quite a bit of editing after the photos have been captured without needing a darkroom or advanced knowledge of how to manipulate film. Editing your photos after they have been captured is called *post production*, or *post* for short.

During post you can make minor tweaks to change how bright your image is, or maybe what colors shine through the most. You can even change the shape and size of the image, or do drastic things like cut major parts of the photo, add images from other pictures, apply filters, and do other fancy things.

Most computers today come with some sort of built-in photo editing software that will help you perform minor edits to color and brightness, and maybe the contrast, size, shape, and so on.

High-end photo editing software such as Portrait Professional and Adobe Photoshop gives you the tools you need to doctor your photos the way the professionals do. These tools will give you the ability to edit your photos all the way down to the pixel. But professional tools come at a professional price.

iPhoto

If you have a Mac, you are in luck because your computer comes with a program called *iPhoto.* iPhoto is a photo management and editing tool. When you plug your drone camera, add-on camera, or SD card into your Apple computer, chances are good that iPhoto will load and give you the option to immediately import your photos. iPhoto also organizes your photos by date. If you would like to organize them yourself, you can do so by creating albums and simply dragging and dropping your imported images into their new home. In addition to the management of your aerial photo collection, iPhoto comes with several tools to edit your photos, shown in Figure 14-5, so they look exactly how you remember them or better. You can save copies of your edits to preserve the originals and easily share the photos from iPhoto with your friends and family via email.

If you ever want to get your aerial images printed, iPhoto also comes with a book-making feature. This features makes it possible for you to arrange your photos in a book and send it to Apple to be printed. In a week or so you'll get a book, made by you, filled with your images. Now *that* is a cool gift for your family and friends, or you.

Chromebook and Pixlr

If you have a Chromebook, you have far fewer options for photo editing than what is readily available on Macs and PCs. But don't fear, your Chromebook comes with a photo gallery manager that will help you organize your imported photos. In the Chromebook gallery, you can view your images, make minor edits to the photos, and even apply built-in color filters. If you need something a little more high-powered, try Pixlr.

Figure 14-5:
iPhoto rocks the photos!

Courtesy of Tucker Krajewski

Pixlr is cloud-based photo editing software. Cloud-based means that you don't need to install anything on your computer, you simply go to the website. If you are on a Chromebook, you can add Pixlr to your Chromebook through the Chromebook app store at no cost. With Pixlr you can easily filter your photos and adjust colors, brightness, and more. Use drawing tools to add in features to your photos or use auto features to make edits like removing red-eye. Figure 14-6 shows Pixlr in all its glory.

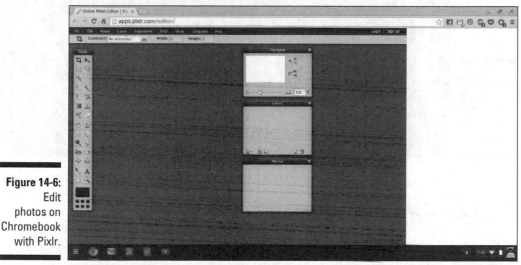

Figure 14-6: Edit photos on Chromebook with Pixlr.

Courtesy of Tucker Krajewski

Adobe Photoshop

Adobe Photoshop has become an industry standard for photographers and photo editors around the world. The term "photoshop" is used more often than not to describe the process of editing photos. Photoshop comes with a seemingly limitless number of features giving you the ability to adjust, edit, create, and modify anything and everything in your image. Built-in filters make it possible to add effects, or simplify common photo editing tasks like sharpening photos to remove blur or softening photos by adding blur. Photoshop must be purchased, and it isn't cheap. But if you are serious about editing your aerial photos, then it will be worth the investment. Figure 14-7 is a picture of Adobe Photoshop.

Adobe has recently made Photoshop, as well as their other multimedia tools, available for purchase on a subscription basis. Sign up for Creative Cloud to gain access to Photoshop for a low monthly fee rather than paying a lump sum to use it indefinitely.

Figure 14-7:
Adobe
Photoshop
is the indus-
try standard.

Video Editing Software

Similar to photo editing, video editing is a process called *post*. In post, video is imported to a computer and then loaded into some sort of video editing software where you can cut out pieces of video, combine parts from different video files, remove or add audio, adjust the colors, brightness, and more. You can even add in special effects or animations with video editing software. Video editing software can range in features and functionality and therefore there are several different types of professional software suites that focus on specific things. Some are specifically for working with video where as others might be for creating and using animations. You will need video editing software if you intend to do anything more than simply viewing your aerial video footage.

iMovie

If you have a Mac, you're in luck because Apple has a free video editing tool called iMovie which is included with almost every Apple computer. iMovie is a basic video editor that gives you the ability to drag and drop your video files into a timeline so that you can align your videos to play one after the other, or you can cut out pieces of your different video files and line the individual video segments in whatever order you desire. iMovie also gives you the ability to edit your soundtrack. Delete the audio in your video files in whole or in part, add sound on top of the existing soundtrack, such as a song or musical score. You can even add sound effects throughout your video. Adjust the colors, brightness, and contrast of your video in whole or in part, add photos, and easily save your new home movie into any number of file formats. iMovie is a great tool for making great home movies. Figure 14-8 is a picture of iMovie. Look out, George Lucas!

If you have an Apple computer, give iMovie a try before spending money on another video editing software.

Adobe Premiere

Adobe has a high-powered video editing tool, called Premiere, that is used by many professional videographers and movie makers around the world. Premiere comes with all sorts of advanced features beyond simple picture manipulation like color, contrast, and brightness. Premiere has numerous advanced features for adding and organizing videos, multi-camera modes, high-end transitions for blending different videos together, slowing down or speeding up video to make video sequences synchronize with audio tracks, and more. Adobe also has other high-end animation software, and audio editing software, all of which integrate seamlessly into Premiere.

If you're planning to make the next Hollywood hit, or if you're wanting to take on the local film competition, Adobe Premiere is a great tool to have in your toolbox. Premiere isn't cheap, but Adobe offers it on a monthly subscription much like their other software products. A word of caution: if you have never used advanced video editing software before, you will definitely need to read some tutorials before you will be able to get up and running with Premiere. Figure 14-9 is a picture of the Adobe Premiere workspace.

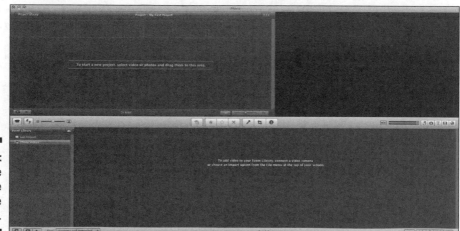

Figure 14-8: Use iMovie to make epic home movies.

Courtesy of Tucker Krajewski

Courtesy of Tucker Krajewski

Figure 14-9:
Adobe
Premiere
is serious
video
editing!

Sharing Pictures and Video Online

Integrated drone cameras and all add-on cameras are going to provide you with great images and videos. With great quality comes big file sizes, however, and big file sizes can be hard to share with your family and friends. You can very easily share your photos and videos over email, however most email services cannot support emails that are over 10 megabytes (MB) in total size. For the most part, the images you capture with your drone's integrated camera or with your add-on camera will be bigger than 1MB a piece. The videos will be even bigger. This all means that while email may be okay for a photo or four, it isn't a reasonable option for sharing much more than that. If you want to share videos and images, you will want to use a cloud-based storage solution. "Cloud-based storage solution" is a fancy way to say "a place on the Internet where you can store your files."

There are several cloud-storage options available to you, but the most popular options are services called Dropbox, Box, and Google Drive. These services offer small storage amounts, usually 5 Gigabytes (GB) or less, for free. If you need much more beyond that, you will have to pay a monthly subscription fee, but it's nominal at best. You can learn more about these services by visiting them online:

✔ **Dropbox:** www.dropbox.com

✔ **Google Drive:** www.google.com/drive

✔ **Box:** www.box.com

Part V
The Part of Tens

Visit www.dummies.com for more great *For Dummies* content online.

In This Part . . .

- ✔ The do's and don'ts of flying drones
- ✔ How businesses can use drones
- ✔ Following FAA regulations

Chapter 15

Ten Things You Shouldn't Do with Your Drone

In This Chapter

▶ Flying your drone safely

▶ Respecting your neighbors' privacy

▶ Avoiding no-fly zones

▶ Minding the law

Although drones have been around for quite some time, the latest innovations in the technology have revolutionized how the world views unmanned, remotely piloted aerial vehicles. Remote controlled flying is no longer for model nerds (no offense if you are a model aircraft nerd). It is slowly making its way into pop culture. In fact, I can probably get my 12-year-old niece, Claire, to fly a drone and think it's the coolest thing since selfies and Instagram. As drone technology continues to evolve, aircraft will fly longer, farther, faster, and more autonomously. Popularity will drive this forward at increasing faster speeds and like all new technology that catapults itself into the mainstream, there needs to be a user manual for common sense.

Remember when Google Glass was all the rage? There were a lot of Jordy LaForge lookalikes "exploring" places like the bathroom, the I-405 from the driver's seat, Sunday Mass, and the dinner table. Very quickly the world began documenting improper usage of Google Glass on the popular social media platform, Twitter, using a hashtag (those phrases you see everywhere that begin with "#") just for the purpose. I'm going on record now with a new term for people that make bad decisions with a drone: #dronehead. Get it? It sounds like "bonehead." Anyway, #dronehead decisions are going to get you in trouble and set the movement behind. Or maybe it will thin the herd like a sort of technological natural selection.

While this chapter isn't intended to be cotillion etiquette training for drone users, it should at least give you a barometer by which you can determine if you are making good decisions with your drone.

Make good decisions, people!

Spying On Your Neighbor

When I was a kid, I used to get on the swing set at kindergarten and try to swing high enough to see over the fence at the back of the playground. There was never anything going on in the neighboring house's backyard, but it was an innocent feat of strength and agility. Flying a drone in the backyard with the hopes of seeing into your neighbor's backyard, while not necessarily illegal, isn't a sweet childhood activity. It's creepy. Currently, there are no laws in place that say you can't fly a drone in your own backyard. But even if it is in line of sight with your neighbor's property, that doesn't mean that you shouldn't be considerate of your neighbors that may feel uncomfortable with being in camera shot of your drone. Not to mention, just because there isn't legal precedent doesn't mean that a #dronehead idea like using a drone to peep into your neighbor's window can't turn into legal precedent when your neighbor takes you to court.

Walk Your Dog

Earlier this year, a video of a drone walking a golden retriever started circulating the Internet. In the video, the dog owner programmed a route for the drone to fly. He then hooked up his dog to the drone with a leash and set the drone off to fly at a reasonable pace. The video was somewhat fabricated but it brought up a great point: Should you use your drone to walk your dog? If you need to automate every aspect of dog ownership, you should probably reevaluate whether or not you should have a dog. That said, unless you have a remarkably well-trained dog, this is not a good idea!

Drones are not powerful enough to guide an animal in any setting. This is not only dangerous to the dog, it's dangerous to other pedestrians and drivers. My 5-year-old cockapoo (actually, he's my wife's) isn't the smartest quadruped. When I walk him, he still manages to get the leash wrapped around light poles, trees, and other objects, causing him to strain against the leash and me to trip. Imagine your drone trying to walk your dog, the dog decides it's time to make a stop, and your drone keeps heading on its programmed path.

You probably get the idea. Until drones get stronger (or more assertive) and artificial intelligence gets a bit better and is integrated into flight controllers, walking your dog is a task that should be carried out in a much more analog manner.

Carry the Ring down the Aisle

People love to watch video of wedding bloopers. Watching the wedding party take a bath in the ocean after a dock collapse, or maybe a bridesmaid loses her balance and falls down, or, in the case of a buddy of mine, you drop the ring in the pool in the middle of the ceremony. Whatever the case is, wedding bloopers are great television. For that reason alone, you should probably *definitely* rig your drone up to be your ring bearer. In all seriousness, however, there are some inherent risks involved with having your drone carry the ring or, even worse, escort your bride down the aisle.

Flying a drone in a crowded area presents several risks, primarily centered around causing bodily harm to the audience. You can't forget that drones are a combination of mechanical and computer components, all of which can fail for various and unforeseen reasons. A drone that is balanced improperly, or goes into an autopilot mode, or has some other malfunction, could crash into someone or something like the ocean. Don't make a #dronehead mistake. Let your best man carry the rings.

Fly in Airport Airspace

Large aircraft are absolutely fascinating to watch take off and land. Commercial aircraft require an unbelievable amount of power to achieve flight, and it never gets boring to watch this feat. Naturally, an airfield is an excellent place to plane spot. Even better, get an up close and personal video and pictures of aircraft landing and takeoff with your drone, right? Not at all. Airspace around an airport is restricted and flying your drone in or within five miles of an airfield would not only be a #dronehead mistake, it would be illegal.

In early 2009, a commercial aircraft took off from New York's LaGuardia airport headed to Charlotte, North Carolina. Within three minutes of takeoff, the plane flew through a flock of geese and a couple of those airborne honkers got into the plane's jet engines. The result was raining ground ganders over the lower east side and the plane had to make an emergency landing. The impact with the geese was so catastrophic that both engines were completely shot and the craft had to crash land with the only reasonable option being the Hudson River. The good news is that the plane landed smoothly and all passengers and flight crew made it off the plane with no lives lost. It was a miracle to say the least.

This sort of scenario is quite possible when you introduce unmanned flight craft into an active airfield. While the resulting video and pictures could be absolutely amazing, the chance of a stiff gust of wind pushing your drone into a plane's flightpath is all too real. Don't be a #dronehead; get up close and personal with binoculars not with your drone.

Flying Under the Influence

The only thing you should be doing if you've had a few too many cocktails is sitting at home and watching television. Along with keeping your car keys out of reach, you should tuck your drone safely away in its storage kit. Flying a drone requires fine-tuned senses, attention to details, and good judgment. No matter how "great" the idea is, there are too many things that can go wrong that can cause harm to your drone, property, or worse, other people. Don't be a complete #dronehead. If you've consumed something that can impair your judgment, don't fire up your drone.

Fly Over the Fences at the White House

There are a ton of great things to see in Washington, D.C. The Capitol building, Washington Monument, the milieu of war memorials, museums, architecture, parks, and, of course, the White House. Don't do it. The area over Washington, D.C., is a strict no fly zone and has been ever since September 11, 2001. Figure 15-1 shows a map of the flight restricted zone (FRZ).

Of course, if you aren't the president or someone in the "inner circle" at the White House, doing anything at the White House other than taking pictures from outside the perimeter fence, is likely to get you into a heap of trouble. Below is the U.S. code that clearly states (in legalese) that your drone is grounded in Washington D.C.

49 U.S. Code § 46307 – Violation of national defense airspace: A person that knowingly or willfully violates section 40103 (b)(3) of this title or a regulation prescribed or order issued under section 40103 (b)(3) shall be fined under title 18, imprisoned for not more than one year, or both.

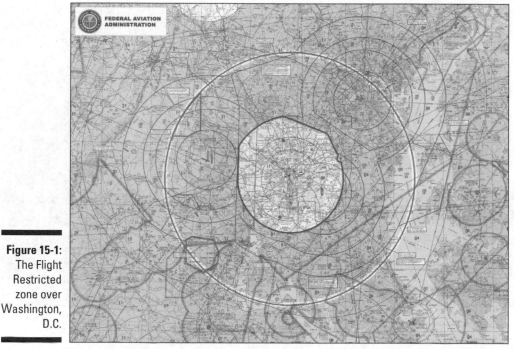

Source: faasafety.gov

Figure 15-1:
The Flight
Restricted
zone over
Washington,
D.C.

So, when deciding if you should or shouldn't fly a drone in or around the White House, don't do it. It's illegal, you will get busted, and it will be a black-eye on the emerging drone community. If you want to make a statement about current laws of the land, walk your drone over to the United States Capitol building and meet with your appointed congressional representative. Or write them a letter.

Checking Extra Batteries on a Flight

If you're passionate about drone flying, you're likely going to want to take your drone with you everywhere you go. If you're driving, you don't have to worry too much about transporting your drone. If you're flying commercial, however, you do need to know how to package and transport your drone.

Almost all modern drones are powered by Lithium Polymer batteries. Lithium Polymer batteries (LiPo), pictured in Figure 15-2, are somewhat dangerous because if not handled properly, they can become damaged and cause fire. In 2010, a UPS flight carrying a cargo container filled with Lithium batteries

Source: Brett Samuel/Creative Commons

Figure 15-2:
Popular types of Lithium Ion and Polymer batteries.

crashed and killed both crewmen on board after the batteries caught fire and filled the plane with smoke.

The good news is that you *can* fly with LiPo batteries, as long as they are carried on. If you need to check your batteries, they must be installed in the device that they are intended to power. This means that you can't simply pack extra LiPo batteries. If you do, and the TSA finds them in your checked bag, they will likely be confiscated.

Shoot Down a Drone

Drones have become a polarizing topic for many people and for many reasons. Opponents to the deployment of lethal drones in combat zones argue that drones cause an excess of civilian deaths, violate international law, create an unhealthy detachment from the horrors of war, and so on. Domestically speaking, people fear the erosion of our right to privacy. So much so that there have been several stories in the news telling of private individuals clearing the skies of drones by any means necessary including shotguns, nets, and other projectiles.

Individuals have argued that drones flying over their property is an invasion of privacy and trespassing and therefore have the right to "defend their property from invasion." The problem is that the airspace above your property isn't technically your property. You can't destroy someone else's drone on grounds (ironic) of trespassing. In fact, you can't destroy someone else's property and not expect to be responsible for replacing it.

For example, if someone were to park their car on your front lawn, you could have it towed and charge the car owner for the expense. But if you were to take a sledge hammer to it or light it on fire, you would be responsible for damaging it.

Note to self, don't be a #dronehead. If you don't want your neighbor flying a drone over your house, be a neighbor and talk to them about it. If the conversation is unproductive, file a complaint with the city.

Fly Over People

There are a lot of public places where you will probably want to get some aerial footage. Concerts, sporting events, amusement parks, and busy city streets are just a few of them. But flying over people presents a lot of risk to the people below. A gust of wind, a bad battery, an inexperienced pilot, falling objects, or any other unforeseen event could cause your drone to come crashing down to earth. If there is a person or people below, you could be in for some problems.

If you are flying recreationally, your best bet is to stay away from crowded areas. If you absolutely must fly where there are people, at least make sure that they know that you will be flying overhead so they can be wary of falling sky. If the weather isn't favorable, or you are a new pilot, don't be a #dronehead, stick to the wide open spaces and get some flight hours under your belt before you venture off into the wild world of civil litigation.

Make Money with Your Drone

Chapter 16 tears into 10 different commercial uses for drones and drone technology. In fact, there are many more ways you can use your drone to make money. From delivering flowers and chocolates to locating parking spaces in crowded mall parking lots, the opportunities are limitless. However, until the FAA releases their rules and regulations (and Congress approves them), the options are actually limited to a few small industries.

For the time being, the FAA is only hearing appeals for commercial uses on a case-by-case basis. Hollywood, naturally, had the juice to get clearance for a handful of film studios to use drones to reduce the costs associated with gathering aerial camera shots for major motion pictures. For everyone else, the front of the line can be a long way off.

In the meantime, to get updates on the status of the FAA rules and regulations, see `https://www.faa.gov/uas`.

Chapter 16

Ten Commercial Uses for Drones

*O*ver the next 10 years, it will be exciting to see how drones will affect life domestically and abroad. Currently, operating a drone for commercial purposes is illegal in the United States. The skies will not officially open to commercial drones until the FAA releases an official set of rules and regulations for commercial drone usage. At the writing of this book, the legislation was pending but has yet to be updated and implemented. In addition, NASA is engineering a system for monitoring and policing drones in American airspace.

This nationwide moratorium on commercial drone usage has created space for numerous companies to get into the drone business by alleviating the need to quickly race a product into the marketplace. If you are thinking about how you might make some money with your drone, consider some of the commercial ideas listed in this chapter.

Real Estate

Real estate is big business all over the world. The buying, selling, and building of property has much to benefit by incorporating drones into the day-to-day business of real estate. Listing agents of residential properties can use drones to create beautiful video tours of their properties inside and out. Using a drone to capture video footage of particularly large properties also makes it easier to capture areas that may be somewhat difficult to reach on foot during a showing. Homebuyers' agents can also use drones to verify the quality and integrity of a home's outside features that would likely require a ladder and a different pair of shoes.

It's not just the buying and selling agents that can benefit from drones; home services companies can benefit, as well. Exterior home inspections can now be performed with a drone, saving inspectors time, energy, and liability. Masons can inspect hard-to-reach stone and brick work to remotely assess the integrity of stones and tuck pointing. Chimney companies and roofers have the same sort of benefit by being able to scan structures without having to set foot on a ladder or lift truck. Drones also make it possible to inspect and document areas that may otherwise get overlooked.

The commercial real estate industry stands to benefit from drones much in the same way as residential real estate. Commercial properties range in size and complexity, from strip malls to high-rise buildings. Drones can help developers inspect buildings without needing to bring in heavy equipment and put humans at risk. Developers and construction companies can also use drones to track construction progress with photos and videos. Drones can also be used for safety inspections, land surveying, and high-quality aerial imagery and videos that would previously cost a small fortune.

Golfing

Serious golfers are always looking for a way to improve their golf game, whether it's the new clubs, special golf balls, shoes that fit and flex just right, or a snazzy pair of pants that make you look amazing while you're cranking your 9 iron. Drones are next in line for innovating the golf game. Drones can be used to gather fantastic video of the golf course for marketing purposes. But beyond that, imagine stepping up to the 4th hole on St. Andrew's old course on the eastern coast of Scotland and being able to review a video of the hole before you take a club from the bag. Using a drone to carefully map out each hole on a golf course can give golfers a unique look at the task at hand.

Golf spectating just got more up close and personal as well. Drones can be used to capture the game in ways that were previously not possible. Forget about blimps and helicopters, golf can take a page out of the Sochi Olympics book and use drones to bring golf to life on television.

Drones can provide great value to golf coaches and pros as they work to improve the golf game of their protégés. Drones can provide photos and videos from a variety of locations, making it possible to more comprehensively analyze a golf swing, chip, putt, or even a victory dance. Figure 16-1 shows a drone being used to give you a better picture of your golfing terrain.

Figure 16-1:
Be a better golfer with a drone!

Source: Ed Schipul/Creative Commons

Drones can also be used to calculate environmental differences at each hole in real time. Temperature, barometric pressure, wind speed and direction, and relative humidity can all impact the golf game. With a drone, you can gather environmental data at green level, and at a variety of variations.

Inspections

Inspections are a big business in many industries. The cost for inspecting can vary greatly depending on the accessibility of the location, the equipment needed to conduct the inspection, and the risk to human life to conduct the inspection. Drones may prove useful for several types of inspections. For instance, oil companies can use drones to inspect pipelines in remote areas. Drones can be programmed to follow the pipeline in an autopilot mode capturing imagery and various sensor data along the way. Drones could also be used to identify and report precise geo coordinates of breaks or other issues with the pipeline.

Wind energy engineers can perform inspections on wind turbines and turbine props without needing to bring in heavy lifting equipment, or put humans at risk of injury. Engineers could also quickly deploy numerous drones to inspect multiple wind energy machines at once. High speed and high-definition inspections mean faster, more efficient inspections without a loss of productivity or risk to human life.

Bridge repairs, bridge maintenance, and bridge construction all require very close inspection by civil engineers to ensure structural integrity. Bridges, however, come in all shapes and sizes. Inspecting a typical interstate overpass is much different than inspecting a suspension bridge over water like the Golden Gate Bridge. A drone can capture high-definition video of every joint, support, crack, and crevice which can be more thorough than what a human engineer on the job might be able to do because of environmental variables and safety restrictions. Video documentation is also good for insurance purposes.

Agriculture

Farming is tricky business because you have to anticipate Mother Nature and be ready to respond on a moment's notice and even then, your response may not make a difference. Giving farmers an additional tool to be able to cope with whatever nature throws at them is a benefit to the world. Drones make it possible for farmers to be able to address hydration issues by measuring water content of soil. This can help farmers identify whether they have drainage issues or irrigation problems. Drones can also be used to help farmers measure how fast their crops are growing in remote fields. Advanced sensors such as LIDAR can measure the distance from plant tops to the ground giving farmers an idea of how crops are progressing throughout the growing season.

Farmers spend big bucks on pesticides to deal with bugs that come in and devastate their crops. Drones can be used to detect the presence of crop-wrecking bugs and then even deploy hyper accurate pesticide applications instead of spraying an entire field. That saves time and money.

Drones aren't just for growing crops; they are also for animal growers. With GPS technology, drones can be used take livestock out to pasture and keep the herd together. Drones can also be used to detect and protect against predators that may be waiting for the opportunity to bag an unsuspecting mammal.

Security

Drone surveillance has already been in the news quite a bit as it has been used to protect the American border with Mexico. Drones have been used to track and apprehend criminals. Drones are also being used in warzones to track fugitives and terrorists. Facial recognition and other advanced technology has greatly aided in military efforts around the world. Back home, securing property with aerial monitoring systems will be a big deal for businesses and institutions of all types and sizes.

Educational institutions have an obligation to students and their parents, staff, and faculty to ensure their safety and security while on campus. Colleges and universities have to deal with crime of all types, especially on urban campuses. Drones can help educational institutions monitor campuses, detect abnormal activity and potential threats, and send help signals immediately to school administrators and law enforcement agencies.

Security is also a major concern for businesses. Major corporations with sprawling campuses in urban centers and small businesses in rural areas all take security seriously. Using drones to provide employee escorts to their vehicles at night, or even providing full-time drone surveillance of parking lots and structures, can help reduce incidents. One-button panic assistance can page drones and simultaneously contact authorities in the event of an emergency.

Weddings & Special Events

The most epic events of your life deserve epic documentation, and drones are the answer. Choosing a wedding photographer has always been a balance of capabilities, qualities, and cost. Well, now you can bet your bottom that drones will make it easier for your photographer and videographer to get the money shots that you and your family are paying for. Drones can be used to get aerial shots that were once unobtainable for the vast majority of couples. Drones also enable you to get beautiful footage of the bride walking down the aisle. Your big day just got more cinematic.

Aerial photography and video of major events such as concerts and sporting events are about to get much better with drones, as well. Suspending cameras from massive wires has been the normal mode of operation for sporting events until now. The 2014 Sochi Olympics was one of the first major sporting events to use drones to capture footage of a live sporting event. Like those awesome shots of the snowboarding and ski slope sports? Those shots were captured from octo-copters (8 blades) like the one shown in Figure 16-2.

Another great use for drones is to capture well-choreographed footage of live concerts. Bands, event producers, record labels, you name it — they can leverage drone technology to capture breathtaking video footage and still imagery of concerts. This kind of footage would normally require renting expensive booms, dollies, jibs, and more.

Figure 16-2:
Great action shots taken by drones.

Source: Ville Hyvönen/Creative Commons

Search and Rescue

In 2005, the southern states of the United States were blasted by Hurricane Katrina. Katrina was a category 5 hurricane when it blasted up against Louisiana, causing 108 billion dollars in damages. The levees in and around New Orleans were overwhelmed, and the city went underwater. The damage was so extensive that it made getting and keeping support personnel on the scene extremely difficult. Clean water, electricity, and food were all scarce, and the damaged roads and high water made it very hard to perform search and rescue for people stuck in their homes in areas that were completely destroyed.

In 2012, wild fires across New Mexico and Colorado ravaged hundreds of thousands of acres of forest, destroying hundreds of homes and displacing many people. More than 1,800 firefighters were brought in, but widespread drought and constantly shifting wind patterns made combating the fires difficult. The area decimated by the fire was so vast and the areas so remote that it made search and rescue extremely difficult, as well.

In 2014, drones were introduced as a critical tool for locating people in areas ravaged by fire, flood, or other natural disaster. Drones can be equipped with sensors like infrared that can be used to locate humans in remote areas by their heat signatures. Streaming video can be used for visual identification of people in distress and GPS information gives rescue personnel the ability to precisely locate the distressed and send in aerial support to rescue people. Lifesaving is getting more and more advanced and successful thanks to drone technology!

Special Delivery

Technology giant Google recently gave the world a sneak peek into their drone project called Project Wing. Due to flight restrictions in the United States, Google has been developing and testing their drone delivery system in Australia. Their custom-built drones take off and land vertically, but then switch orientation to fly more like a glider or plane, which gives them a greater flight distance. Google envisions their Project Wing initiative will help deliver supplies to humans in remote areas of the world like the Australian outback or rural areas of Third World countries that lack the infrastructure needed to get deliveries in and out expediently.

Google isn't alone in their push to create a fleet of drone delivery vehicles. E-commerce giant Amazon has also announced that they are developing and testing their own fleet of drones for offering product deliveries. The grand vision is same-day service for packages under a certain weight. Amazon's aerial package delivery system will be loaded with a delivery and programmed with GPS coordinates and then using advanced imaging technology, the drone would lower the package to a safe location like a front porch or driveway. The service would give customers the ability to track their package in flight as it travels the skies to reach them.

Of course, these are nothing more than high-flying dreams until the new FAA regulations for commercial drone use in America are updated and released.

This framework will also impact drone usage around the world as the FAA's regulations impact many countries. Currently, legislation is in process but will take time to open up enough to support the grand visions of American entrepreneurs.

More important than package delivery and transporting supplies to remote areas, how about never having to tip the pizza delivery guy again? When the new regulations are released, you better believe the world will need piping hot pizza delivered by an UAPDV (unmanned aerial pizza delivery vehicle).

Land Surveying

Land surveying is a big business and entirely critical for anyone that is building any sort of structure or preparing an area of land for a specific use or establishing property boundaries. You've probably seen land surveyors as you've been going about your business where ever you live. Figure 16-3 shows some site surveyors. Surveying requires crew, gear, and heaps of time especially if the land mass being surveyed is particularly vast.

Drones, however, have made it possible to do site surveying more accurately and in less time. Drones can be programmed to fly over hundreds of acres,

Figure 16-3:
Site
surveyors
surveying
land with
traditional
means.

Source: Elvert Barnes/Creative Commons

take pictures and video, map elevation changes with LIDAR or other sensors, locate water and water flow patterns, detect the presence of different minerals and resources, you name it. The information can be analyzed and processed in shorter time because the process is automated with drones.

In addition to saving time and money, drones also reduce the risk that humans experience when surveying remote and treacherous land. Drones can be programmed with coordinates to stay within a specific area and can survey all the hard to reach places in remote areas.

Insurance Claims

Have you been in a car accident recently? They are terrifying, embarrassing, and costly — and that's before you get insurance involved. You wait for days sometimes until your insurance company sends someone out to inspect your damage. With new technology, you could notify your insurance company of your accident using a mobile app on your phone. The app could then transmit information including coordinates back to the insurance company whom could then take your coordinates and dispatch a drone to come out and gather pictures and video of the accident scene. The information could then be used to get the insurance claim process started much faster.

Drones aren't just for car wrecks. If you're a home owner, you may be terrified (or thrilled) when you hear or see a thunderstorm barreling down on the homestead. Thunderstorms can produce winds that can bring down trees, and hail that can destroy your roof and your car. With drones, your insurance inspector no longer needs to climb onto your roof to inspect damage, or to get aerial imagery of a tree that fell on your garage. Drones can come in to document your damage with photos and video and speed the process up while reducing risk of accident on the insurance inspector. Less liability to their employees means lower insurance for you, right? Probably not. But at least the claim process will go faster.

Chapter 17

Ten FAA Regulatory Implications

*I*n Spring 2015, the FAA released a set of proposed rules and regulations to govern the commercial use of drones in the United States. The original set of rules did not carve out any real plan or course of action for the commercial use of drones, which has caused quite a bit of ruckus. In fact, the rules actually made it even more difficult for businesses to be able to use drones for business. The rules are confusing; they are still changing and will likely be constantly changing as drone use expands and evolves. This chapter provides ten tips for staying in line with some of the changing FAA regulations for commercial use.

Commercial versus Personal Use

One of the biggest points of contention in drone regulation is how and when a drone can be used for commercial purposes. Currently, you cannot use a drone for commercial reasons without acquiring special approval directly from the FAA. There is, however, some gray area in defining *commercial use*. To provide clarity for what is considered commercial versus personal use, the FAA released an interpretive document (FAA-2014-0396) which outlined some specific use case comparisons. Here are a few examples of personal drone use that were outlined, in case you want to ensure that the way you are using your drone is considered personal:

- ✔ Flying your drone to take pictures for personal use is considered hobby use. A realtor using a drone to take pictures of a property they have listed, are in process of listing, or intend to list, is considered commercial use.

- ✔ Flying your drone at local model aircraft club is considered hobby use. Flying your drone for demonstrating, teaching, or performing in exchange for money is considered commercial use.

- ✔ Using a drone to move a box from one point to another without any compensation is considered hobby use. Delivering packages for a fee is a commercial use.

- ✔ Viewing a field of crops to determine density, water needs, and so on is a hobby use as long as the crops are being used for personal enjoyment or consumption. Using your drone to view your crops that you are growing for sale is considered a commercial use.

If you have any doubt surrounding how you use your drone, and whether or not the usage would be considered commercial or personal, do this basic test: Am I generating money from these activities whether directly or indirectly? If the answer is yes, you are using your drone commercially.

Getting Approval for Commercial Use

It is currently illegal to operate a drone for commercial uses unless you receive specific authorization from the FAA. In February of 2015, the FAA released a blanket approval for using drones for commercial use; however, to get this clearance you must apply for an exemption, and the FAA still reserves the right to deny exempt status. To apply for a Certificate of Waiver or Authorization, you must go to the FAA website (www.faa.gov) and complete an online application. If you are awarded and exemption, you still must adhere to strict guidelines which include:

- ✔ Total unmanned aircraft weight must not exceed 55 lbs.

- ✔ Flight altitudes are limited to 200 feet or lower.

- ✔ Flights must be conducted during the day.

- ✔ The unmanned aircraft must remain in line of site at all times.

- ✔ The unmanned aircraft must be at least 5 miles away from an airport with a functioning air traffic control tower.

- ✔ Your unmanned aircraft must registered with the FAA.

If your usage falls outside of these parameters, you can apply for a special Certificate of Waiver or Authorization online here (`https://oeaaa.faa.gov/oeaaa/external/uas/portal.jsp`).

Getting Approval For Public Use

Government agencies can use a drone for governmental purposes if the drone is owned by the government agency or is on exclusive lease for a period of no less than 90 days, and it is being operated for crew training or demonstration purposes only. For any other use, the government agency is required to secure a Certificate of Waiver or Authorization from the FAA. The agency can apply online here (`https://oeaaa.faa.gov/oeaaa/external/uas/portal.jsp`). Once the application is reviewed and conditionally approved, the FAA will work with the agency to determine a geographic boundary and parameters for the usage of the drone. The FAA will want to ensure that the use will not be in a populated area and will not interfere with manned commercial flights. The COA is typically issued for a period of time that doesn't normally exceed two years. If you work for a state or local government agency and you want to use a drone, make sure you follow the rules or you may find yourself in a political hot seat.

Gaining Experimental Certification

Several large companies in the United States have been working toward developing commercial drone technology even though the regulations governing commercial drone usage have not relaxed enough for big business to take to the skies. Google has been testing their Project Wing initiative in Australia simply because it was easier to get up and running there than it has been in the United States.

Recently, the FAA rolled out a special certification for organizations that are working on developing unmanned aircraft and need to be able to train ground crew, test technology, and perform demonstrations. This special certification can be acquired by applying directly to the FAA (`http://FAA.gov`). The FAA reviews each request on a case-by-case basis and then upon approval of the request, the FAA works closely with the applicant to clearly define usage restrictions, including geography, type of aircraft, manner in which it will be used, and so on.

Amazon recently petitioned the FAA and was awarded a certificate to be able to test their experimental delivery drones. The FAA required that Amazon provided rigorous reports on number flights, pilot duty time per flight, malfunctions, anything unusual and any deviations from air traffic controller's instructions. While this doesn't solve the bigger issues at hand, it does at least bring company testing back to the U.S.

Capturing the News With a Drone

The FAA frequently asked questions (FAQ) page specifically calls out whether news organizations can use a drone to capture the news, and the answer is no. Using the drone to capture the news, while it doesn't directly generate revenue, is deemed to be a commercial use for the drone. Now there are legal ways that news organizations are working around this restriction, and with good reason. Drones are a valuable tool for news agencies because they capture footage that would otherwise be unattainable without a news helicopter. In April and May of 2015, a series of horrendous earthquakes occurred in Nepal that caused massive amounts of damage and great loss of life. News organizations were able to capture the magnitude of the damage with the aid of drones. There is no denying that drones are a useful tool for the newsroom.

News organizations can enlist the services of a third party with no official affiliation with news agency to capture footage for them assuming the third party has FAA clearance. This footage could then be used for broadcast and would not be in violation of the FAA rules and regulations. Also, if drone footage is captured without the intent of selling it to a news agency, the footage can be serviced and broadcast. Seems a bit ridiculous but hey, the story isn't going to tell itself, right?

Knowing the Proposed Commercial Drone Rules

The FAA previously has not allowed any sort of commercial uses for unmanned aerial vehicles. However, the new proposed regulations have loosened this stance but it still provides tight restrictions on how a drone can be used for business purposes. Following is a list of some of the changes:

- The unmanned aircraft must weigh less than 55 lbs. (25 kg).
- The unmanned aircraft must remain within visual line of sight of the operator or visual observer (spotter) unaided by any device other than contact lenses or glasses.
- The unmanned aircraft cannot be flown over people or vehicles

✔ Usage of the unmanned aircraft is limited to daylight-only operations (official sunrise to official sunset, local time).

✔ Must yield right-of-way to other aircraft, manned or unmanned.

✔ Maximum airspeed of 100 mph (87 knots).

✔ Maximum altitude of 500 feet above ground level.

✔ Minimum weather visibility of 3 miles from control station.

✔ No operations are allowed in Class A (18,000 feet and above) airspace.

✔ Flight above 500 feet requires special permission from air traffic control.

✔ No person may act as an operator or VO for more than one unmanned aircraft operation at one time.

✔ The unmanned aircraft must undergo a preflight inspection by the operator.

✔ A person may not operate a small unmanned aircraft if he or she knows or has reason to know of any physical or mental condition that would interfere with the safe operation of a small UAS.

My favorite proposed rule states that you may not be careless or reckless with your drone.

Knowing the Proposed Rules for Commercial Drone Operators

Not only did the FAA propose new regulations for Drones, but also for drone operators. That's right, if you are going to fly a drone for commercial purposes, there are specific rules governing how to obtain certification to be a legal commercial drone operator. Following is a list of these items:

✔ A commercial drone operator (operator) must pass an initial aeronautical knowledge test at an FAA-approved knowledge testing center.

✔ Operators must be vetted by the Transportation Security Administration. This is a security background check to ensure that you are not on any sort of watch list.

✔ Operator must obtain an unmanned aircraft operator certificate with a small UAS rating (like existing pilot airman certificates, never expires).

✔ Operator must pass a recurrent aeronautical knowledge test every 24 months.

✔ Operator must be at least 17 years old.

✔ Operator must make available to the FAA, upon request, the small UAS for inspection or testing, and any associated documents/records required to be kept under the proposed rule. Check out Appendix A for a sample flight log that can be used to track all of your flight time.

✔ Operator must report an accident to the FAA within 10 days of any operation that results in injury or property damage.

✔ Operator must conduct a preflight inspection, to include specific aircraft and control station systems checks, to ensure the small UAS is safe for operation.

Under the proposed rules, it will not be as simple as buying a drone and charging your batteries. There are several rules designed to keep you and the people around you safe when using your drone for commercial purposes. One key reason why these rules are so rigorous for commercial operators is because the assumption is that commercial operators will operate their drones with greater regularity than hobby flyers. This means more regular congestion in the air which can mean greater chance of incident. The ruling will be made official before 2016.

Following Drone Privacy Laws

The FAA's proposed regulations for drone usage primarily centered around commercial uses of drones and commercial drone operators. The proposed regulations did not offer any suggested solutions for privacy concerns that have been arising across the country. EPIC (Electronic Privacy Information Center) petitioned the FAA to establish drone privacy rules prior to releasing revised commercial regulations. Now EPIC has taken the battle one step further by suing the FAA stating that the FAA failed to implement privacy rules that were mandated by the FAA. That doesn't mean that there are no rules whatsoever governing how and what you can do with your drone. Each state has begun hearing and passing laws to protect individual rights of privacy from other individuals including officials and law enforcement. To stay on top of drone legislation, go to the American Civil Liberties Union website at `http://ACLU.org`.

Understanding the Proposed Regulations for Micro Drones

Several countries, like our neighbor to the north, have created regulation classes for drones based on size and weight. There has been extensive study done on the potential dangers of aircraft collision with small to medium size birds. The findings determined that small birds caused no life-threatening damage to aircraft at or below an altitude of 400 feet. So it is assumed that a small and lightweight drones are not a safety hazard either. For this reason, the FAA is considering drafting a MicroUAS class of regulations for drones that fit certain criteria. Proposed regulations include to govern micro drones include:

- ✔ The micro drone must weigh less than 2 kilograms (4.4 lbs)
- ✔ The micro drone must be made out of fragile material that can break on impact
- ✔ The micro drone must not move faster than 30 nautical miles
- ✔ The micro drone must not exceed 400 feet above the ground
- ✔ The micro drone must only be flown within the operators sight and the operator must control the plane by sight and not through automated controls.
- ✔ The micro drone must remain 5 miles away from any airport.

The proposed regulations are very similar to existing regulations governing drone usage. The primary differences have to do with the weight of the drone, the material that it is comprised of and the speed at which the drone moves.

Helping with FAA Enforcement

It is important for the all drone operators to adhere to the rules, regulations and laws set forth by the FAA. Currently the FAA is not staffed for policing drone usage to ensure adherence to federal regulations. Therefore, they rely heavily on civilians and local law enforcement to keep an eye out. The FAA suggests that "first responders" take the following steps to help them enforce the law:

- ✔ Locate witnesses and gather statements on what they witnessed.
- ✔ Gather evidence like video footage or photos.
- ✔ Document how the drone was used and whether or not it was within a restricted area.
- ✔ Contact a regional FAA operational office.

If the FAA receives notice of reckless use of a drone, they may attempt to contact the operator by sending and educational letter. If the letter is not sent from the FAA legal department, you don't have to sweat to hard. Make sure you read the letter and glean what you can. If the letter is sent from the FAA legal affairs, you may want to pay close attention to see if there is any sort of action being taken. Not responding to these letters can be lead to automatic judgments like fines. The rule of thumb is to play by the rules!

Appendix A

Flight Log

· ·

*T*he FAA regulations will continue to evolve as the world of drones continues to grow and mature. For that reason, it's a good idea for you to keep records of your flights, regardless of whether the flight is for fun or work. It's also nice to be able to have a written record of your flights for historical purposes. Keeping a flight log will also be helpful in the event you have flight control issues on a future flight or possibly even some damage that you need to diagnose. Your flight log will help you track the life of your battery and keeping meticulous records is also a good way to cover yourself in our increasingly more litigious culture. You may also find that as there more jobs become available for experienced drone pilots, your log will be your record to prove your history of flying.

The flight log contained in this appendix is a generic form with space to add additional information in a comment field. The log covers two pages of information which include:

- ✔ **Date:** This is the date of the flight. Include month, day and year.

- ✔ **Flight number:** If the current flight is your tenth time flying a drone, then place a 10 here.

- ✔ **Drone type:** Include the make and model of your drone. For instance, a DJI is the make, Phantom Vision+ 2 is the model.

- ✔ **Drone ID:** This is your drone's unique ID.

- ✔ **Take Off:** Where did you take off from? This could be GPS coordinates or a quick description.

- ✔ **Landing:** Where did you land? This could also be GPS coordinates or a quick description of where you landed.

- ✔ **Weather:** Be descriptive. If you can, include air pressure, precipitation, clouds, temperature, wind, and humidity.

- ✔ **Distance:** The distance you flew in miles or kilometers.

- ✔ **Maximum altitude:** How high did you go at your highest point?

- ✔ **Comments:** This is a great place to give a short narrative for your flight. Include any unique maneuvers learned, crashes, close calls, remarkable pictures or video, close calls with collisions, or simply whether it was a calm, relaxing cruise. Document your memory of this flight so that you have more things to jog your memory if you ever want to recall it.

- ✔ **Start time:** This is the time that you armed your drone for takeoff.

Arming your drone means that your drone is on and ready to fly. Do not touch your drone once it has been armed. If your drone is in an advanced flight mode and you move the drone, it could cause the drone to think that it needs to correct it's orientation. This could lead to a propeller injury.

- ✔ **Stop time:** This is the time that you landed your drone and disarmed it.

- ✔ **Total:** The total flight time from start to stop.

Last but not least, after you fill up a page of entries, sign it and total up the time so that you have a handy quick reference to use when you need to recall flight details. You can find a copy of this flight log on this book's website (www.dummies.com/extras/drones).

Flight Log

Date	Flight Number	Drone Information		Flight Location		Flight Conditions	Flight Specifics	
		Drone Type	Drone ID	Takeoff	Landing	Weather	Distance	Max Altitude

(continued)

Comments	Piloting Time		
	START	STOP	TOTAL
	Total Hours On This Page		
	Total Hours To Date		
	Signature		

Date	Flight Number	Drone Information		Flight Location		Flight Conditions	Flight Specifics	
		Drone Type	Drone ID	Takeoff	Landing	Weather	Distance	Max Altitude

(continued)

Comments	Piloting Time		
	START	STOP	TOTAL
	Total Hours On This Page		
	Total Hours To Date		
	Signature		

Index

• *X* •

• *Y* •

About the Author

Mark LaFay has entrepreneurialism running through his veins. From grade school to now, LaFay has created and run small businesses that have taken him and his products around the world. LaFay built businesses in the music industry, producing hundreds of events in Central Indiana and developing numerous musical acts into internationally touring and recognized groups. LaFay is co-founder of Lectio (http://mylectio.com), a software startup and mobile application built to encourage independent reading for students with language related learning disabilities; he's a minority owner and board member of Social Net Watcher, a tech company helping schools and parents combat bullying; and he is a co-founder of Roust, a social network for people interested in discussing politics, policy, religion and social issues. LaFay is an adjunct professor in the school of informatics at IUPUI (Indiana University, Purdue University, Indianapolis) and the author of *Chromebook For Dummies* (Wiley).

Dedication

I dedicate this book to my beautiful, loving wife, Carrie LaFay, and my amazing son, Harvey Clayton LaFay.

Author's Acknowledgments

In the middle of writing this book, my amazing wife and I welcomed our first son into the world. Harvey Clayton LaFay was born on December 17, 2014, in Indianapolis, Indiana. Writing a book when you want to play with your newborn is a tough thing. I have my dearest Carrie LaFay to thank for her support. I also must thank my brother in-law, Paul Thrift, and his better half, Angie Thrift, for letting Carrie and me invade their space so that I could write. Thank you to the editing staff at Wiley for having me on for another book and making sure I sound smart. Last and definitely not least, thank you to TJ Johnson from Airdroids (maker of the pocket drone). This book would not have been possible without you.

Publisher's Acknowledgments

Sr. Acquisitions Editor: Katie Mohr

Project Manager: Colleen Diamond

Development Editor: Colleen Diamond

Copy Editor: Colleen Diamond

Technical Editor: TJ Johnson

Editorial Assistant: Claire Brock

Sr. Editorial Assistant: Cherie Case

Production Editor: Vinitha Vikraman

Cover Photo: © iStock.com

DRONELIFE·com

The Premier Source for Drone News

The commercial drones industry is the new wild west of technology; there is a lot of money to be made, unclaimed territory to be mapped, and there are hardly any rules.

DRONELIFE is here to make sure you, the consumer, are up to date on all the latest drone news, product releases, YouTube videos and legal precedents so you can stay informed about the rise of the commercial drone.

DRONE NEWS

DJI Releases Firmware, Mobile App Updates for Phantom 2 Series

DJI, makers of the increasingly popular Phantom line of commercial drones, released on Wednesday updates for the Phantom 2 firmware and VISION mobile app (for iOS and Android). The full list of new features...

SkyWard Announces Urban SkyWays Project to Demonstrate the Potential of UAVs

As with most emerging technologies, it is difficult for anyone to fully understand what a drone brings to the table until they see it in action. This is why Portland-based SkyWard announced on Tuesday the Urban SkyWays Project.

Introducing Atlanta Hobby's New Vortex Drone

3D Printed in America. That is the first thing AtlantaHobby.com wants you to know about their latest release, the Vortex drone. The frame of the drone is 3D printed on aerospace-grade 3D printers which means the UAV is both durable and light at the same time.

Dummies products make life easier!

- DIY
- Consumer Electronics
- Crafts
- Software
- Cookware
- Hobbies
- Videos
- Music
- Games
- and More!

For more information, go to **Dummies.com**· and search the store by category.

FOR
DUMMIES
A Wiley Brand